THE
BIBLE IN PICTURES
FOR LITTLE EYES

To Michael

from Uncle Bob

12 - 31 - 98

Books by Kenneth N Taylor
THE BIBLE IN PICTURES FOR LITTLE EYES
DEVOTIONS FOR THE CHILDREN'S HOUR
STORIES FOR THE CHILDREN'S HOUR
LIVING BIBLE (Tyndale House Publishers)

ISBN: 0-8024-0896-6

Printed in Singapore
Worldwide Co-edition organised and produced
by Angus Hudson Ltd, London

THE
BIBLE IN PICTURES
FOR LITTLE EYES

Introduction

VEN LITTLE CHILDREN can understand great truths when told to them in simple words. And when pictures are added, doubly indelible impressions are made that can last forever.

No other book has changed so many lives so remarkably as the Bible. God's Word can be a source of light to childhood's earliest pathways if carefully presented. It can be a Rock to build a life on, even when that life is very small. "Give us a child until he is five years old," some say, "and his character will be formed forever."

It is incredibly important to begin *direct* Bible training at the earliest possible age, in addition to the influences surrounding the child from earliest days in a Christ-honoring home. This book can be read to children of approximate asges 3½ to 6 with great profit. Children of that age can understand with simple trust the great doctrines of God and His dealings with mankind. With simple trust they can accept and always believe what hardened, older minds find difficult.

It is the hope of author and publisher that this book will be a means of establishing little minds in truths from which nothing that will ever happen in the years ahead can shake them, because their trust will be in the Living God and in His Son, Jesus Christ our Lord.

CONTENTS

NEW TESTAMENT

The Old Testament
in Pictures for Little Eyes

HEN IT IS NIGHTTIME and the lights are out you know how dark everything gets. You can't see anything. That is how all the world once was. There were no pretty flowers; there were no trees or grass or birds. There were no children either. There was only darkness. God did not want everything to be all dark. He decided to make some people. People could not live in the darkness so God made a beautiful world full of light.

QUESTIONS:

1. *Can you see anything at night when you go to bed and the lights are out?*
2. *Did God want everything to be all dark?*

Genesis 1:2-5

HIS IS THE BEAUTIFUL WORLD God made. How different it is from the cold, dark picture we looked at before! Now the world is warm and bright and pleasant. The animals are playing and everyone is happy. God has made all these things and all of them are very good but there are no people anywhere. God has not made any people. All the pretty things are here but there are no people to enjoy them, so God will make some people to live here.

QUESTIONS:

1. *Can you see a lion in this picture?*
2. *Can you see any people?*
3. *Did God decide to make some people?*

Genesis 1:1

HESE ARE THE PEOPLE God made. Can you see them in the picture? They are behind the flowers in the middle of the picture. Can you point to them? The man's name is Adam. The lady's name is Eve. Adam and Eve did not have a mother and father. God made them out of dust from the ground, and then He made them become alive. God made them happy and good. They love God and God loves them. In the picture you see them looking up toward God. No wonder they are so happy.

QUESTIONS:

1. *What is the man's name?*
2. *What is the lady's name?*
3. *Did Adam and Eve have a mother and father?*
4. *Who made Adam and Eve?*

Genesis 2:7-9

ADAM AND EVE are not happy now. Do you know why they are so sad? It is because they have been bad. They did something God told them not to do. God told them they could eat anything except the fruit from one tree. God told them not to eat that one kind but they could eat all the other kinds. The tree was so pretty and the fruit on it looked so nice that Eve wanted to eat it, but God said, "No." Then Satan, who is God's enemy, told Eve to eat it even if God said not to. Eve took the fruit and ate some of it; then she gave some to Adam and he ate it too. Now God is punishing Adam and Eve. He is sending them out of the beautiful garden and they can never come back again.

QUESTIONS:

1. *Who are these two people?*
2. *Where are they going?*
3. *Why can't they stay in the garden?*

Genesis 3:8-13

HESE TWO MEN are Adam and Eve's children. See how big and strong they are! Once they were little children but now they have grown up. Do you see the one with the lamb? His name is Abel. God told them both to bring lambs to give to God, but only Abel is bringing a lamb. Can you see what his brother is bringing? Is he bringing a lamb? God told him to bring a lamb. Is he obeying God? No, he is not. God does not like this, because he is bringing some things from the garden instead of bringing a lamb. This bad brother's name is Cain. Cain got angry with Abel because Abel did what God said and brought God a lamb. And then, do you know what Cain did? He hit his brother Abel and hurt him so much that Abel died. God will punish Cain for killing Abel. Cain killed his brother Abel because he was angry at God. What a terrible thing to do!

QUESTIONS:

1. *Which of these two men is Abel?*
2. *Which is Cain?*
3. *What did God say to bring?*
4. *Point to the one who is obeying God.*

Genesis 4:8-13

THIS MAN'S NAME is Noah. Can you say his name? I am glad to say that this man loves God very much. He wants to do whatever God tells him to do. He is a good man. God has told him to build a big boat. It is so big that it takes him a long, long time to build it. Can you see the big boat he is building? See how hard he and his sons are working! They are working so hard because God has told him to build the boat and he is happy to do whatever God says. Do you know why God wants Noah to have a boat? It is because God is going to send so much rain that all the ground and the houses will be covered with water, and if he does not have a boat he will die. The waters would go over his head and he would drown, but if he is in the boat he will be safe and dry. God is going to take care of Noah and his family and keep them safe and dry.

QUESTIONS:

1. What is this man's name?
2. What is he doing?
3. Why is he building the big boat?

Genesis 6:13-22

T LAST NOAH'S BOAT is all finished. Can you see the boat in the picture? It is away in the back, over by the sun. See how nice the boat looks! Now it is time for Noah and his family to go into the boat. God tells Noah to take a mother and daddy lion with him into the boat. He tells him to take a mother and daddy bear too. A mother and daddy of every kind of animal are going into the boat because that is what God said. In the picture you can see all the animals going into the boat. Maybe all the other people laughed at Noah for believing that God would make it rain so hard, but Noah didn't care. He believed God and got into the boat. Then God sent the rain.

QUESTIONS:

1. *Where are all the animals going?*
2. *Who told the animals to get into the boat?*
3. *Why did God want the animals in the boat?*

Genesis 7:6-17

FTER NOAH AND HIS FAMILY and the animals all went into the boat God sent the rain. It rained and rained, all day and all night, and for many days and nights. Down and down the rain came until all the flowers and bushes were covered up with water; soon all the houses and trees and people were covered up with the water too. Noah and his family are safe in the boat where God is taking care of them. The animals are safe too. The bird you can see in the picture is a dove that was inside the boat. Noah let it go out to see if it could find a home, but now it is coming back to the boat because of the water.

QUESTIONS:

1. *Where are the flowers and houses?*
2. *Where is Noah and his family?*
3. *Where are all the other people in the world?*

Genesis 8:8, 9

OW HAPPY NOAH and his family are! They are not in the boat any more. Now at last the water has all gone away and the ground is dry again. Now Noah and his family have come out of the boat onto the dry land. They can see the grass again and the flowers and trees. Now the little children can run and play. Can you see what Noah is doing? He is praying to God. God is glad because Noah is praying. God says He will never again punish bad people by sending so much rain to kill them. God put a rainbow in the clouds because of His promise. Do you see the rainbow in the picture? Have you ever seen a rainbow outside your house? Whenever you see a rainbow it is God telling you that He loves you.

QUESTIONS:

1. *Who are these people?*
2. *What are they doing?*
3. *What is that up there in the sky?*

DO YOU SEE the high building the men are making? Why are they making this high building? They are making it because they do not like God. They want to make a high building to prove that they are very great. They think that they are greater than God! God does not like this. He will not let them make the building. He will make them talk so funny that they cannot understand each other. They will not be able to tell what their friends are saying. Then they will stop building the tall tower because they cannot talk to each other and cannot tell each other how to help. This building is called the Tower of Babel.

QUESTIONS:

1. *What are the people building?*
2. *Why are they building it?*
3. *What will God do?*

Genesis 11:1-9

ERE IS A PICTURE of a very important man. His name is Abram. Sometimes he is called Abraham. Abraham is a very good friend of God. God loves him and he loves God. God told him to take a long, long trip, to go far, far away and live there the rest of his life with his wife and his helpers and his camels and his sheep and his cows. Abraham said, "Yes," to God. He told God he would go wherever God wanted him to. Abraham loves God. He is God's friend.

QUESTIONS:

1. *What is this man's name?*
2. *What did God tell him to do?*
3. *Did he do what God said?*

Genesis 12:1-9

ABRAHAM IS TALKING to his friend whose name is Lot. They are talking about where to live. Abraham has many sheep and so does Lot. Sheep eat grass for their breakfast and lunch and supper. There is not enough grass here for Abraham's sheep and Lot's sheep too. Abraham is saying to Lot, "There isn't enough grass here for all our sheep. Only one of us should live here. One of us should go somewhere else to live where there is more grass. You go where you want to live and I'll take my sheep and live somewhere else." Lot is telling Abraham that he wants to live where the grass is long and green and best, so that his sheep will have plenty to eat. He wants the best grass. Lot is being selfish. He wants the best things for himself. After Lot has taken his sheep and gone away, God will give the best land to Abraham. Abraham isn't selfish, so God will give him the best.

QUESTIONS:

1. *Who are these two men?*
2. *What are they talking about?*
3. *What did they decide?*
4. *What will God tell Abraham?*

Genesis 13:5-18

BRAHAM IS SAD. He is sad because he has no children. He needs a little boy. He talked to God about this. He asked God to give him a son. God tells Abraham to come outside with Him and look up into the sky at night and count the stars. But Abraham can't count them. There are too many to count. God says, "Abraham, I am going to give you a little boy and when he grows up he will have children and pretty soon there will be so many children that you won't be able to count them. You can't count the stars and you won't be able to count all the children and their children that I will give you." Now Abraham is happy because God will give him a little baby boy. God is glad because Abraham believed Him. Abraham knows that God will not fool him. He knows God will do just what He says.

QUESTIONS:

1. *What is Abraham looking at?*
2. *How many children did God say He would give Abraham?*
3. *Did Abraham believe God?*

Genesis 15:1-7

38

ABRAHAM HAS BECOME very old. See how old he is! Sarah, his wife, is old too. They are too old to have a baby. But God promised that He would give them a little boy. Three men have come to visit Abraham. Can you see them in the picture? When Abraham saw the three men he ran to meet them even though he was so old and the afternoon was so hot. Abraham knew that the three men had come to visit him from Heaven. He asked them to come and eat with him and they did. They had a picnic under the trees. These men told Abraham that Sarah his wife was going to have a little baby. Sarah is laughing because she does not believe that God can give her a baby. But God will do just what He said. Soon God will give a baby boy to Abraham and Sarah. How happy they will be then! The baby's name will be Isaac.

QUESTIONS:

1. *Where did these three men come from?*
2. *What did the three men tell Abraham?*
3. *Why is Sarah laughing?*

Genesis 18:1-15

GOD GAVE ABRAHAM a little baby boy just as He promised. Now in this picture you can see that the baby has grown to be a big boy. He is with his father Abraham and his father is very sorry. Do you know why the father is sad? I will tell you why. It is because God has told Abraham to bring Isaac here and to kill him. God wants to know if Abraham loves God best or loves his boy best. Abraham loves his boy very, very much, but of course he loves God the very best of all. Soon Abraham will take out his knife to kill his dear son. Then suddenly God will call to Abraham and say, "Stop, Abraham, stop! Don't do that. Don't hurt him. Look behind you!" Abraham will look and see a lamb caught in some bushes. "Kill the lamb," God will say. "Don't kill your son. I know now that you love Me." The lamb will die so that Abraham's big boy can come home again with his father. Now the father is glad.

QUESTIONS:

1. *What did God tell Abraham to do?*
2. *Why did God say this?*
3. *Who did Abraham love most, God or his dear boy?*
4. *Who do you love best?*

Genesis 22:1-18

Do you see the man talking to the nice lady? Do you know what they are talking about? The man is asking the lady where her father is. He wants to talk with her father. The man has come a long way. He lives with Abraham in another country. Abraham told him to go and find a wife for his son Isaac. The man asked God to help him find the right lady. This is the lady God will give to Isaac to be his wife. The man will ask the lady and her father if she will be Isaac's wife and they will say yes. The lady's name is Rebekah. She will be Isaac's wife.

QUESTIONS:

1. *What is the man talking to the lady about?*
2. *Who sent the man to talk to the lady?*
3. *Will the lady go with him to be Isaac's wife?*

Genesis 24:10-26

HIS IS THE GIRL who said she would be Isaac's wife. Her name is Rebekah. You can see Isaac running toward her. She has come on the camels for a long, long way to be his wife. She has never seen Isaac before, and Isaac has never seen Rebekah before. They are happy because God has given them to each other. Soon God will give them two babies. They will have twins, named Jacob and Esau.

QUESTIONS:

1. *What is this girl's name?*
2. *Who is running toward her?*
3. *What will their children be named?*

Genesis 24:63-67

OW ISAAC HAS BECOME very old, and soon he will die. His two baby boys have grown up now and one of them is kneeling down in front of him. It is Jacob who is kneeling there. Jacob is not a baby now—he has become a big man and his father is very old. Jacob is telling his father a lie. His father cannot see very well because he is so old. He thinks it is his other boy who is kneeling there. He does not know that it is Jacob. The father wants to give some nice things to his other boy and Jacob says that he is the other boy; so now the father will give the nice things to Jacob. Jacob wants nice things. He tells a lie to get them.

QUESTIONS:

1. *What is Jacob telling his father?*
2. *Why did Jacob tell a lie?*
3. *Who does the father think is kneeling there.*

Genesis 27:1-2

OW JACOB IS TAKING a long walk to another country. His father has told him to go there to find the girl who will marry him. Jacob is tired and is lying down to sleep because it is night. He is having a dream. Have you ever had a dream? Jacob dreams that he sees stairs or a ladder that is so high that it goes right up into the sky. Angels are going up and down the ladder. Then in his dream Jacob will see God standing at the top of the ladder and telling him that many wonderful things will happen to him because God loves him.

QUESTIONS:

1. *What is Jacob doing?*
2. *Where is he going?*
3. *What is his dream?*

Genesis 28:10-1

ACOB IS NOW a long, long way from home. He is in another country. He is helping a girl whose name is Rachel. She is taking care of her father's sheep. While he is talking, Jacob finds out that the girl is a friend. She invites him to come to her house. Her father will be glad to see Jacob. He will let Jacob and Rachel get married. Jacob will live in that country with Rachel. He will not go home to his father for a long time.

QUESTIONS:

1. *What is this girl's name?*
2. *Who is she talking to?*

Genesis 29:1-12

52

ACOB IS WRESTLING with an angel, but they are not trying to hurt each other. Jacob wants to win so that the angel will give him many nice things. The angel touches Jacob's leg so that he cannot use it very much, but Jacob will not stop wrestling. The angel wants to stop but Jacob won't let him. Jacob is saying, "I will not let you go unless you bless me." Then the angel said he would give him many wonderful things. Afterward Jacob knew that the angel was God. God blessed Jacob and gave him many presents.

QUESTIONS:

1. Who is Jacob wrestling with?
2. What did Jacob want?

Genesis 32:24-30

GOD TOLD JACOB to move to another house with his wives and children. God told Jacob to go home to his father and visit him. Here you can see them taking a long trip to their new home. The children will be glad to see their grandfather. In this picture you can see their father Jacob talking to their uncle Esau. Their father is afraid of Uncle Esau, but Uncle Esau is kissing him. A long time ago their father had been bad and had stolen something from Uncle Esau. They thought their uncle might try to hurt them because their father had done this. But their uncle is very kind. In the picture you can see him hugging their father.

QUESTIONS:

1. *Are Jacob and Esau fighting?*
2. *Why is Jacob afraid of Esau?*
3. *Where are the children going?*

Genesis 33:1-4

56

HIS BOY WITH THE PRETTY COAT is Joseph. He is talking to his father, Jacob. Jacob loves Joseph very much. Joseph is seventeen years old and is helping to take care of the sheep. His father has given him the pretty coat as a special present because he loves him so much. The little boy is Joseph's brother. His name is Benjamin.

QUESTIONS:

1. *What is the boy's name who has the pretty coat?*
2. *Who gave him the coat?*
3. *Who is the little boy?*

Genesis 37:3

WM. E. FAY

OSEPH IS GOING for a long walk to find his brothers and the sheep. His father is asking him to go and find them. Joseph is glad to help. He is telling his father, "Good-by." He will find the brothers and the sheep. But the brothers aren't nice. They don't like Joseph because their father gave Joseph the nice coat. They are angry at Joseph. They will try to hurt him. Isn't that too bad?

QUESTIONS:

1. *Who is Joseph talking to?*
2. *What does his father want Joseph to do?*
3. *Will Joseph's brothers be glad to see him?*

Genesis 37:13-2

JOSEPH HAS FOUND his brothers. But what is happening to him? Can you see him in the picture? He is the one without a shirt. Two men are taking him away. His bad brothers are selling him. Do you see the man paying money to one of the brothers? The man is buying Joseph. The cruel brothers are happy because they do not like Joseph. Now Joseph will be taken far away to another country. He can't go home to his dear father any more because his brothers have sold him and the men who bought him are taking him away. But God is with Joseph and it will be all right.

QUESTIONS:

1. *Which one in the picture is Joseph?*
2. *Where are they taking him?*
3. *Why is the man giving money to Joseph's brothers?*

Genesis 37:28-36

OSEPH IS IN ANOTHER COUNTRY far away from his home. But God is there with him and everybody likes Joseph very much. He works hard and he always does whatever is right. The man Joseph works for likes him a lot. He has made Joseph his most important helper. In this picture you can see Joseph telling the other men what to do.

1. *Is Joseph at his own house?*
2. *Does everybody like Joseph?*
3. *What is Joseph doing?*

Genesis 39:1-

64

OOR JOSEPH! He is in jail. Do you see the bars on the windows so that he cannot get out? He must stay there for a long time. He has not been bad, but someone told a lie and said that he had been bad. But God is with Joseph there in jail. God is taking care of Joseph even when he cannot get out. The other men in the jail like Joseph. He tells them things that are going to happen to them. God helps Joseph know what is going to happen, and he tells the other men.

QUESTIONS:

1. *Where is Joseph?*
2. *Can he get away?*
3. *Is Joseph telling the men what is going to happen to them?*

Genesis 39:20-2

JOSEPH IS TALKING to the great king. Everyone is afraid of the king. He has very much money and can tell everyone else what they must do. If they do not do what he says, he will hurt them. But the king is not happy. Do you know why? It is because he had a bad dream last night. He dreamed about some cows. The cows were fat and some other cows that were thin came and ate up the fat cows! Someone told the king that Joseph could tell about the dream and why the cows did this. Joseph was in jail but the king let him out. In this picture you can see Joseph telling the king about the dream. Joseph says that God sent the dream to the king. God wants the king to know that pretty soon there wouldn't be enough grass for the cows and they would all get very thin and hungry. God tells Joseph about the dream, and then Joseph tells the king.

QUESTIONS:

1. *What did the king see in his bad dream?*
2. *Who is talking to the king about the dream?*
3. *Who told Joseph what the dream meant?*

Genesis 41:1-13

THE MAN SITTING DOWN behind the horse is Joseph. All the people are nice to him. They like Joseph. Why do all the people like him? It is because the king has made Joseph his most important helper. Now everyone must do what Joseph says, or else the king will punish them.

QUESTIONS:

1. Who is the man everyone is looking at?
2. Do the people have to do what Joseph tells them?
3. Do you know who Joseph's best friend is?

Genesis 41:14-16, 38-44

HERE IS ANOTHER PICTURE of Joseph. He is sitting on a golden chair. The other men are his brothers. Do you remember how bad his brothers were? Do you remember that they sold him? They have not seen Joseph for a long long time. They do not know it is Joseph they are talking to. They are afraid of this man because he is so rich and so great. They have come to ask this man for food because they are hungry. These are the bad men who hurt Joseph. They sent him away when he was a little boy. Joseph knows that they tried to hurt him. Do you think that Joseph will give them food? Yes, Joseph loves his brothers even though they were so bad, and he will give them the bread they are asking him for.

QUESTIONS:

1. *Who is the man sitting down?*
2. *Who are the other men?*
3. *Why did they come?*
4. *Will Joseph give them bread?*

Genesis 42:6-

OSEPH IS TELLING the bad men that he is their brother. These men thought that Joseph was dead, but he is alive and talking to them. God has made Joseph rich and strong so that he can help his brothers and his father now that they are hungry. The brothers were bad to Joseph and made him go away, but God was with Joseph all the time and took care of him. Now Joseph is taking care of his brothers. He loves them anyway, even if they were so bad. Do you know that God loves you, even when you are bad and even when He must punish you?

QUESTIONS:

1. *What is Joseph telling the men?*
2. *Did God take care of Joseph?*
3. *Will Joseph hurt his brothers because they hurt him?*

Genesis 45:1-1

THIS OLD MAN is Joseph's father, whose name is Jacob. Jacob is very, very old now. He knows that God will soon take him away to Heaven. Jacob is talking to Joseph, and to Joseph's two boys. He is asking God to be kind to these two boys. Jacob is blessing the two boys and praying to God about them. He is asking God to take care of them and help them.

QUESTIONS:

1. *Who is this old man?*
2. *Where is he going to go soon?*
3. *Who is he talking to?*
4. *What is he saying to them?*

Genesis 48:9-

WHAT IS HAPPENING to these people in this picture? They are working very hard. One man is being whipped. A man wants him to work harder, and that is why he is whipping him. These people who are working so hard are God's people. They are called the children of Israel. Does God know what is happening to them? Yes, and God will help them. He will send a helper. In the next picture you will see who God's helper is going to be.

QUESTIONS:

1. *What is the name of these people?*
2. *What is happening to the man?*
3. *Does God know about this?*
4. *What will God do?*

Exodus 1:7-1

78

SEE THE LITTLE BABY! Why is his mother putting him in the little boat? She is putting him there because the king wants to hurt the baby. The mother is hiding him. The baby's name is Moses. When the baby Moses grows up into a big man, he will make the king of Egypt stop hurting God's people, the children of Israel. The baby will grow up and be God's helper. God is taking care of Moses by telling his mother to put him into the boat. Moses' sister will watch to see that the baby is all right.

QUESTIONS:

1. *What is the baby's name?*
2. *Why is his mother putting him into the boat?*
3. *Will the baby be God's helper when he gets to be a big man?*

Exodus 2:1-

SEE WHAT IS HAPPENING to the baby Moses. Some nice ladies were walking along and saw the little boat. The lady looking at the baby is the king's daughter. She is the king's big girl. She wants to take the baby Moses home with her and take care of him. She will take the baby Moses to her house and Moses will live there with her. God is taking care of the baby Moses.

QUESTIONS:

1. *Who found the little baby?*
2. *Is God taking care of Moses?*

Exodus 2:5-

82

OW THE BABY MOSES is a big man. He is taking care of some sheep. But now God does not want Moses to take care of sheep any more. Instead He wants him to go to help God's people, the children of Israel. God wants to keep the other people from hurting His children with their whips. God is talking to Moses about this. Moses cannot see God talking to him, but he sees a bush that is on fire. The bush burns and burns, but does not burn up. Can you see the fire in the picture? God is in the burning bush and talks to Moses from there. Moses is hiding his face, for he is afraid to look at God.

QUESTIONS:

1. *Where is the baby Moses now?*
2. *Who is Moses talking to?*
3. *Where is God in this picture?*

Exodus 3:1-

MOSES AND HIS BROTHER AARON are talking to the king. They tell the bad king that God wants him to let the people alone and not hurt them any more. But the king laughs at Moses and Aaron. He will not stop hurting the people. He will hurt them even more. He tells Moses and Aaron to go away and stop bothering him. Then Moses and Aaron say that God will hurt the king if he doesn't stop hurting God's people. All the water in the mud puddles and in the rivers will become blood. Even what is in the glasses on the tables for lunch will become blood, too. God will do this to the king to make him stop hurting His people.

QUESTIONS:

1. *Where is Moses?*
2. *Who is Aaron?*
3. *What are they telling the king?*

Exodus 5:6-1

HO ARE THESE PEOPLE? What are they doing? These are God's people. They are doing what God has told them to do. God said to take the blood of a lamb and put it on the sides of the doors of their houses, and on the board at the top of the door. Why did God want them to put the blood there? God is going to send an angel and in every house that does not have the blood on the door the oldest boy will die.

QUESTIONS:

1. *What is the man putting at the side of the door?*
2. *Why is he doing this?*
3. *Did the king put the blood on the door of his house?*

Exodus 12:1-1

88

IT IS THE MIDDLE OF THE NIGHT and outside everything is all dark. In this picture everyone is crying. Do you know why? It is because the king's oldest boy has died. God's angel came and the boy died because there was no blood on the door. God said to put the blood on the door, but the king wouldn't do it. The king is sorry now that he hurt God's people. He is sorry that he did not believe God and do what God said. Now he will quickly send someone to tell Moses that he will stop hurting the children of Israel. He will tell Moses to take God's people out of his country so that God will not kill any more of his people.

QUESTIONS:

1. *Why is everyone so sad?*
2. *What will the king tell Moses now?*

Exodus 12:29-3

GOD'S PEOPLE are going on a long trip, but they do not know where to go. Only God knows where He wants them to go. God is leading them to a good country. God has sent a big cloud that moves along in front of them. They are following the cloud. God moves the cloud and the people go wherever it goes. At night the cloud becomes fire so that the people can follow it through the darkness. That is how God tells them where to go.

QUESTIONS:

1. *How do the people know where to go?*
2. *Who makes the cloud move?*

Exodus 13:21, 2

EE WHAT MOSES is doing now! God ha told him to stand there by the big rive How can all of God's people get across The water is too deep, and they do no have any boats, and there is no bridge. How can they g across? Moses lifts up his hand, and see what happens All of a sudden there is a path right through the water s that all of the people can walk through. God has tol Moses to do this. God is taking care of His people so tha they can get away from the bad king who wants to hur them. God is very kind to His children. He is kind to you too.

QUESTIONS:

1. *What is Moses doing?*
2. *What happens when Moses does this?*
3. *Does God love His children?*
4. *Does God love you?*

Exodus 14:21-3

WHAT IS HAPPENING in this picture? Can you see Moses standing there? He is holding up his stick and now the water is coming to cover up the bad king and his soldiers. God pushed the water away so His people could walk through the sea on dry ground. They are safe now. Do you see them there behind Moses? The king chased after them with his soldiers but when he was right in the middle, God let the water come back and the soldiers drowned. You can see the water beginning to cover them up. But God's people are safe behind the cloud that God sent to help them.

QUESTIONS:

    1. How did God's people get through the river?
    2. What is happening to the soldiers?

Exodus 14:26-

127

ERE ARE GOD'S PEOPLE out in a field. Th are the children of Israel. What are th picking up from the ground? I don't thir you could ever guess! They are pickir up cake that God has dropped down from the skies that they can pick it up and take it home and have it f their breakfast. There are no stores to go to, to buy foo and so God has sent the food to them. God is very kind His children. He fed His people this way every mornir and at night he sent birds that tasted like chickens f God's people to eat for supper.

QUESTIONS:

1. *What are these people doing?*
2. *Where did the cake come from?*
3. *What did God send the people for supper?*

Exodus 16:

MOSES IS HITTING A ROCK with his stick. Why is he doing this? He is doing this because God told him to. God said that if he would hit the rock with his stick all of sudden water would come out of the dry rock and there would be a river for God's people to drink from. They were thirsty and wanted to drink, and there wasn't any water, so they started crying about it. They said mean things to Moses. Moses asked God what to do. God told him to hit the rock and water would come out. Now the people have all they want to drink.

QUESTIONS:

1. Were the people thirsty?
2. What does Moses have in his hand?
3. How did the water get there?

Exodus 17:1-

THIS IS ANOTHER PICTURE of Moses. See what he is carrying in his hands! He has two big pieces of flat stone. These stones have things written on them. God wrote on these stones and gave the stones to Moses. What does the writing say on the stones? It tells what God wants His people to do. It says to love God and obey Him. No one should ever pray to anyone but God. It says on the stones to take care of our mothers and daddies and do what they tell us to do. Another rule God gives is that we should never take anything that does not belong to us. These rules are written on two stones. There are ten rules so we call these rules the Ten Commandments.

QUESTIONS:

1. *What does Moses have in his hands?*
2. *What are the ten rules called?*
3. *What is one of the rules on the stones?*

Exodus 32:15-1

O H, OH, OH! What are these people doing? These are the people of God, but they a praying to a baby cow. Do you see th baby cow in the picture? They have mad the cow out of gold and now they are praying to it. The people are disobeying God and making God very sorr God says we must only pray to Him. These people a praying to something else. Now God must punish thes people because they are so bad. Moses is very angry be cause the people are doing this. He is throwing down th two stones and breaking them.

QUESTIONS:

1. *What are the people praying to?*
2. *Who is the only One we ought to pray to?*
3. *What is Moses doing?*

Exodus 32:1

104

HE BUILDING YOU SEE in this picture is a kind of church. It is the place where the people of Israel can come and pray to God. Moses is there talking to God. There is a big cloud at the door of the church. The Lord is in the cloud and He is talking to Moses. You and I cannot talk to God in a cloud. But we can talk to Him right here in the room. And He sees us even though we cannot see Him.

QUESTIONS:

1. *Where is Moses?*
2. *Where is God?*
3. *What are they doing?*

Exodus 33:7-1

SEE ALL THE PEOPLE COMING! See what they have in their hands! Some of them are bringing money and some of them are bringing beautiful cloth and some of them are bringing perfume. They are bringing all kinds of things. Do you know why? It is because God has told them that they could bring these things and build a beautiful house for God to live in. They are giving these things to God, and then some of them will help Moses make the beautiful house. The people are happy because they can give these presents to God for His house.

QUESTIONS:

1. *What are the people bringing?*
2. *Why are they bringing these presents?*

Exodus 35:4-29

108

IT IS NIGHTTIME and some of the childre of Israel are looking at the beautif house they have made for God. Is th house on fire? No, it is not on fire, b there is a big cloud of fire there above the house. Do yo know who is in the fiery cloud? It is God. God is watchir over His house. He is taking care of all the people Israel in the tents that you can see. Whenever the fire b gan to move away, then the children of Israel took the tents with them and followed the fire until it stoppe That is the way God told them where He wanted them go when it was nighttime. In the daytime He sent a clou for them to follow.

QUESTIONS:

1. *Is the house burning up?*
2. *Who is in the cloud?*
3. *Where do all the people live?*

Exodus 40:34-

CAN YOU SEE what these men are carrying It is a great big bunch of grapes on a pole The grapes are so big and so heavy tha the men can hardly carry them. The found the grapes far away in another country. God tol them to go there. They found the grapes and brough them home for all their friends to see. God wants thes people to take a long trip to that other country, where th grapes are so big and live there. But the people are afrai to go. They think the men who live in that other countr will hurt them, so they are afraid. They forget that Go will take care of them.

QUESTIONS:

1. *What are the men carrying?*
2. *Where does God want His people to go?*
3. *Are the people afraid to do what God says?*

Numbers 13:23-

GOD TOLD HIS PEOPLE to listen to Moses, b[ut] some of them said they wouldn't mir[d] Moses any more. God is very angry wi[th] these men. God tells everyone to get awa[y] from them, because He is going to hurt them. Then all [of] a sudden the ground opens up and there is a big hol[e]. They fall down into the ground, along with their hous[es] and their friends, and everything that they own. Then th[e] earth closes up again and they are all killed.

QUESTIONS:

1. *Did these men mind Moses?*
2. *What did God do to them?*

Numbers 16:23[ ]

AN YOU SEE all the snakes in this picture
Do you know why they are biting th
people? It is because the people hav
been bad again. So God has sent thes
fiery snakes to bite the people, and many of them are dy
ing. These people have come to Moses. They say, "W
have been bad. Please ask God to take away the snakes.
So Moses prayed for the people and the Lord told him t
make a brass snake and put it on a pole. Moses took
hammer and some brass and made a snake. It isn't a rea
snake; it isn't alive. God tells Moses that anyone wh
looks at the snake on the pole would get well again. Th
people in the picture are looking at the brass snake on th
pole. Now they will be all right. But if anyone won't look
he will die.

QUESTIONS:

1. *Have the people been bad again?*
2. *How is God punishing them?*
3. *What has Moses made?*
4. *What will happen to the people who don
   look at the snake?*

Numbers 21:5-

116

MAN IS RIDING ON A DONKEY and there is a angel standing in front of him with a lon knife in his hand. The angel wants th man to stop because the man is going t do something bad and the angel doesn't want him to. Th man didn't see the angel at first but the donkey did. Th donkey is afraid of the angel and stops. The man is angr because the donkey stops. He hits the donkey and tells to go on. Then the Lord makes the donkey talk, and th donkey asks the man, "Why are you hitting me?" Ju: then the man sees the angel standing there. The man i falling down on the ground because he is so scared. Th man's name is Balaam.

QUESTIONS:

1. *What was the man going to do?*
2. *Can this donkey talk?*
3. *What did it say?*
4. *Why is the man falling off his donkey?*

Numbers 22:21-

118

OSES IS SITTING DOWN on the rock. He is very old man now. Soon he will go awa to die. He will go away to live with Go He will not be with the people of Israe to take care of them any more. So now God is giving th people another leader. Now Joshua will take care of then Joshua is talking to the people and telling them what do. Moses tells Joshua to help the people obey God.

QUESTIONS:

1. *Where is Moses going?*
2. *Who will take care of his people now instea of Moses?*

Numbers 27:18-

120

THIS MAN IS RUNNING FAST. Do you see th other man running after him with a bi knife? The first man is running into th city. He was chopping some wood wit an axe and had an accident. His axe hit a man wh was standing near and the man died. Then he started run ning away to this city and the other man chased him. Yo can see that he is all tired out. But now he comes to th city and the other man cannot hurt him here. God mad this city so that people could run there and be safe. No he is safe.

QUESTIONS:

1. *Why is the man running?*
2. *Where is he going?*
3. *Will he be all right now that he is in the cit*
4. *Can the man with the knife hurt him now?*

Numbers 35:9-

I N THIS PICTURE you can see one of God
people talking to his family. He is tellin
them about God. He wants them to kno
how good God is to him and how kin
God is. He is teaching his children about God so th
when they grow up they will always want to do whatev
God says. He wants his children to love and obey Go
even now while they are still young. God always wan
fathers and mothers to tell their little children about th
Lord Jesus. That is why I am reading these good storie
to you—so that you will know more about God.

QUESTIONS:

1. *What is the man telling his family?*
2. *When you become grown up, what will yo
tell your children?*

Deuteronomy 6:7-

HESE PEOPLE are bringing gifts to God. They want to give them to God because they are so glad God has been kind to them. The grapes are from their own gardens. Do you see the baskets of grapes? See how many there are! They are taking the first of these grapes and are bringing them to God's house for the priest or minister to use. They will give some to poor people who do not have enough to eat.

QUESTIONS:

1. *What is in the basket?*
2. *Where is the man taking it?*
3. *Why does he want to give the grapes to God?*

Deuteronomy 26:1-

OSES IS ON A MOUNTAIN. He is standing on the top of the mountain. He is looking over to the country that God will give the children of Israel. Moses cannot go there because once he did not mind God. God said that he would have to be punished by not getting to go to the nice country. But God will let him see the promised land. God is showing it to him now. God tells Moses to come up to this mountain so that he can look at it. In a little while Moses will die and God Himself will put Moses' body in the ground. But Moses will go to live with God while his body is there in the ground.

QUESTIONS:

1. *Where is Moses looking?*
2. *Will Moses go to the country where he is looking?*
3. *What is going to happen to Moses?*

Deuteronomy 34:1

I T IS NIGHT OUTSIDE. A man is climbing down from a high window. Soon another man will come down too. A lady is helping them. These two men do not live here. They live in another country. They live with Joshua and God's people. God told them to come here and see this city. The name of the city is Jericho. When these two men came to the city, the people who lived there tried to catch them, but the lady is helping them get away. God will be kind to the lady because she is helping these two men.

QUESTIONS:

1. *Do these two men live here?*
2. *Did God tell them to come?*
3. *What did the people try to do to them?*
4. *Who helped them get away?*

Joshua 2:1-1

OD IS DOING A WONDERFUL THING for His children. He wants them to go across the river to the land He said He would give them. There is no bridge for them to go across, and no boat, and the water is too deep to wade. But God makes a way for them to go across. See how the water is standing up like a wall! Now there is a path through the bottom of the river for the people to walk on. The ground is dry beneath their feet. Look at the priest walking ahead of the people of Israel and carrying God's little house. God is making the water stand up instead of getting the people all wet.

QUESTIONS:

1. *How did the people get across the river?*
2. *What is happening to the water?*
3. *Who fixed the river so the people could walk across the bottom of it?*

Joshua 3:13-17

GOD'S PEOPLE are walking around the big cit called Jericho. God has told His people t walk around it every day. They have a ready walked around it once yesterday They have walked around it once every day this week Today God told them to walk around it seven times in stead of once. Now the people are yelling very loudly an the priests are blowing their trumpets. The high walls at falling down, and now all of God's people can walk righ into the city. The people in the city built high walls t keep them out, but God is knocking down the walls. Th is the city where the lady lives who helped the two me climb down the wall. The people of Israel do not hu this lady when they go into the city because she was kin to them.

QUESTIONS:

1. *What are the people doing?*
2. *What is happening to the walls?*

Joshua 6:1-

134

DO YOU KNOW who this man is? He is Joshua, the leader of God's people. God's people are having a great fight with some other people. In the picture you can see all the men fighting. The sun is beginning to go down and it will soon be dark. Joshua and God's people will not be able to see to fight. In this picture Joshua is talking to God about the sun. He is asking God to keep the sun from going down. He wants it to stay where it is so that it won't get dark for a long time. God is listening to Joshua's prayer. There will be no night at all on this day. It does not get dark because God is keeping the sun up there in the sky. God listens to Joshua and doesn't let the night time come.

QUESTIONS:

    1. Did Joshua want it to become dark?
    2. What did Joshua ask God to do with the sun?

Joshua 10:6-1[

136

HY ARE THE MEN drinking water? Some them are putting their mouths into t water and drinking like dogs. Others a putting the water into their hands. Th will drink out of their hands. Can you tell which ones w drink from their hands? God told Gideon to tell the m to drink the water. He told Gideon to choose the m who drink out of their hands. Gideon will take these m with him to fight with the people who don't like God. I will send all the other men home. God only wants a fe men to go. There will not be enough men, so God w help them. God will help them and they will win.

QUESTIONS:

1. *Did God want Gideon to take lots and l of people with him to fight?*
2. *What are the men doing?*
3. *Which ones did Gideon ask to go with hi*

Judges 7:

THIS IS A PICTURE OF SAMSON. Samson is the strongest man who ever lived. He is strong because God made him that way and helped him. God said that as long as he did not cut his hair he would be strong. Do you see his long hair? Here is a picture of Samson and some heavy doors. They are the doors to keep people from going in and out of the walls of that city he is looking at. The doors are shut, and Samson wants to go out. He does not have the key, so he goes out anyway and just takes the doors along with him! What a strong man Samson is!

QUESTIONS:

1. *What is the man's name?*
2. *Did he have the keys to the door?*
3. *How did he get out?*

Judges 16

140

THE STRONG MAN, SAMSON, has chains on his feet. Can you see the chains? How did they get there? I will tell you. One night when he was asleep some men cut off his long hair. Then Samson wasn't strong any more. The men put chains on him and made him blind by hurting his eyes. But now Samson's hair has grown long again and he is stronger. He asked the men to let him stand by the two posts that held up the house. He is pulling the house down and Samson and the people will all die.

QUESTIONS:

1. *What did the men do to Samson's hair?*
2. *How did Samson get the chains on his feet?*
3. *What happened after Samson's hair grew out again?*

Judges 16:18-

HIS DEAR MOTHER is going away. Now she will live somewhere else in another country far away. She is saying good-by to Ruth. But Ruth doesn't want her to go by herself. Ruth wants to go with her and take care of her. Ruth is kind and good.

QUESTIONS:

1. *Is Ruth kind and good?*
2. *Will she go away from the mother?*
3. *Does she want to take care of her?*

Ruth 1:8

144

THIS IS A PICTURE of Ruth. Do you remember how kind she was to her mother? Now she is working hard to get food for both of them to eat. Do you see the wheat in Ruth's hands? She will use it to make bread to eat.

QUESTIONS:

       1. Who is this lady?
       2. What does she have in her hands?
       3. What will she do with it?

Ruth 2:5-1

ANNAH IS PRAYING. She is praying because she does not have a baby, and she wants one very badly. She and her husband have come to the church to pray and to give gifts to God. The minister sees her praying. He tells her that God will answer her prayer. God will send her a little baby because of her prayer.

QUESTIONS:

1. Why was Hannah praying?
2. What does the minister tell her?

I Samuel 1:9-

GOD GAVE HANNAH a little baby boy. Yo
can see him in the picture. The little boy
name is Samuel. Samuel was a tiny bab
but he grew and grew and now he is no
a baby any more. Hannah wants to give her little boy t
God. She has brought him to the church to be a helper t
the minister whose name is Eli. The little boy Samuel
talking to Eli. Samuel's mother will go home now an
Samuel will not see her very much. He will live with E
and be God's helper.

QUESTIONS:

1. *What is this little boy's name?*
2. *Who will Samuel stay with now?*
3. *What will he do?*

I Samuel 2:18,

T IS NIGHTTIME and Samuel has bee asleep. Now he is awake. Now he i awake and listening to someone talking He hears someone calling "Samuel! Sam uel!" The little boy thinks that Eli is calling him from th next room. He runs quickly to Eli and says, "Here I an you called me." But Eli says, "No. I didn't call you. "Who called me, then?" Samuel wants to know. Eli tell him that God was talking to him. Samuel will listen t what God says, and do it.

QUESTIONS:

1. *Was Eli calling Samuel?*
2. *Who was calling him?*
3. *What is Samuel going to do?*

I Samuel 3:1-

ELI IS SITTING ON A ROCK while a man is telling him what has happened. God's peopl[e]
have been fighting with some bad me[n]
called the Philistines. The man is tellin[g]
Eli that God's people are all running away, and that Eli['s]
two sons have been killed. Now Eli is very sad. The ma[n]
tells him that God has let the Philistines win the figh[t.]
When Eli hears this he falls off the rock he is sitting o[n]
and he is hurt so badly that he dies.

QUESTIONS:

1. *What is the man telling Eli?*
2. *Is he telling him happy things?*
3. *What happened to Eli when he heard abou[t]
   it?*

I Samuel 4:5-

THE LITTLE BOY SAMUEL is now an old, ol man. Samuel is pouring oil on the head o a young man whose name is Saul. Go has chosen Saul to be king over His peopl Israel. See how tall and strong Saul is! See how he is knee ing there in front of Samuel! Samuel is pouring some o on Saul's head because Saul is going to be the king. I looks like he will make a good king for all of God's peopl to mind. But do you know something that is very sad? will tell you what it is. Saul's heart has sin in it. Tha means that Saul will do wrong things.

QUESTIONS:

1. *What is the name of the young man?*
2. *Is he good?*
3. *Why is Samuel pouring oil on his head?*

I Samuel 9:15-

THIS FINE YOUNG MAN is David. He take care of sheep. When a lion came to catc David's sheep, David killed the lion. Ca you see the lion lying there under h knee? David is strong and good and God is going to le him be the king over His people. God wants Samuel t pour oil on David's head now, so that David will kno that he is going to be the king.

QUESTIONS:

1. *What is the name of this young man?*
2. *Does he take care of sheep?*
3. *Will he become king?*

I Samuel 16:1-1

A GIANT HAS COME to fight against God['s] people. The giant's name is Goliath. A[ll] the men of Israel have run away fro[m] him. They are afraid to fight him becau[se] he is so big but David is not afraid. David knows th[at] God will help him. David does not have a gun but he h[as] a sling shot. Do you see it in his hand? He takes son[e] stones and uses his sling shot to throw a stone at the gia[nt.] The stone hits the giant in the head and the great Golia[th] falls over dead.

QUESTIONS:

1. *What is the giant's name?*
2. *What did David hit him with?*
3. *Why were all the other people afraid [of] Goliath?*

I Samuel 17:38

DAVID AND JONATHAN are talking together. They are good friends and like to talk to each other. Jonathan is King Saul's son. He is a prince. But Jonathan will never be the king because God has told David to be king. Does this make Jonathan sad and angry? No, Jonathan loves David and he is glad that David is going to be the king. Do you see David and Jonathan talking together in the picture?

QUESTIONS:

1. *What are the names of these two men?*
2. *What is the name of the one who is going to be the king?*

I Samuel 20:4-

HE MAN WHO IS ASLEEP is King Saul. H
has been chasing David. He wants t
catch him so that he can hurt an
kill him. Saul does not like David. H
knows that God is going to make David king instead c
him. Saul wants to keep on being king but God won't le
him. David and a friend with a spear find King Saul sleep
ing. David's friend wants to kill King Saul with the shar
spear. But David is good and he won't let his friend hur
King Saul. David knows God would not like this. Davi
only wants to do whatever God tells him. David mind
God.

QUESTIONS:

1. *Can you see King Saul?*
2. *What is he doing?*
3. *Can you see David in the picture?*
4. *What is he doing?*

I Samuel 24:1-

OW SAUL IS DEAD. David is the new king. The old man is pouring oil on his head. He is doing this to make David a king because that is what God said. Now everyone must mind King David. God told David long time ago that some day he would be king and now he is.

QUESTIONS:

1. *Who is the king now?*
2. *Did David know he was going to be king?*
3. *What is the old man doing to David.*

II Samuel 2:1

DAVID IS BRINGING HOME the golden Ark. anyone looked into the Ark he would di The Ark belongs to God. David is happ that the Ark is coming. He is walkin along in front of it playing on his golden harp. Everyor is happy. God is coming to live with them.

QUESTIONS:

1. *Is David happy?*
2. *What happens to people who open the gold box?*

II Samuel 6:12-

168

THIS IS A PICTURE of King David. In the Bible there are many songs that David wrote and played on his harp. In this picture you can see him playing and singing. The music is very pretty and the words are nice because they tell how much he loves God. Some of the words he wrote are:

"The Lord is my Shepherd,
I shall not want.
He maketh me to lie down in green pastures.
He leadeth me beside the still waters."

QUESTIONS:

1. *What is the name of this man?*
2. *What is he doing?*
3. *Where are some of his songs written down?*

Psalm

THE MAN WITH THE CROWN on his head
King David. God has sent Nathan th
prophet to talk to him. See how he
pointing his finger at King David and ho
David is afraid. David has done a very bad thing and Go
saw him do it. God sent Nathan the prophet to tell Davi
that God is going to punish him. David is sorry that h
has been so bad and asks God to forgive him. God forgiv
David but he will punish him very much for the ba
thing he has done.

QUESTIONS:

1. *Which of these men is King David?*
2. *Has David been good or bad?*
3. *Who sent the other man to talk to Kir
   David?*
4. *Did God punish David for being bad?*

II Samuel 12:1-

172

THIS MAN who is getting caught up there in the tree is Absalom. Absalom is David's son. He is a prince because his father is the king. Absalom doesn't want his father to be king any more because he wants to be king instead. God does not like this. God wants David to still be king. Now look at Absalom. He is caught in the tree. His donkey is running away. He has been riding on the donkey but now he will hang there by his hair because it has gotten all tangled up in the tree and he cannot get down. Soon some men will come who do not like Absalom. He will not be able to get away from them and they will kill him. Now Absalom cannot be the king. God does not want him to be king.

QUESTIONS:

1. *What is happening to Absalom?*
2. *Can he be king?*
3. *Did God want Absalom to be king?*

II Samuel 18:9-

ING SOLOMON is telling two ladies what to do. They have come to ask him what to do with the little baby they are holding. Each of the ladies says that the baby is hers. One of them is telling a lie. Which one is it? God tells Solomon how to find out. He says to cut the baby in half and give half of it to each of the ladies. Then the baby's mother says, "No, no, let the other lady have the baby. Don't cut it in half." Then Solomon knows the lady who doesn't want the baby hurt must be the baby's mother. Solomon gives the baby to his mother. God made Solomon very wise.

QUESTIONS:

1. *Did the baby's mother want him to be hurt?*
2. *Who made Solomon wise?*

I Kings 3:16-

ING SOLOMON built this new house. Do y
know who he made it for? It is Go
house. It took a long time to build it b
cause it is so nice. Many men have c
down trees and made them into boards and other men c
big rocks and worked very hard. Solomon is glad becau
he could make this beautiful house for God to live in.

QUESTIONS:

>1. *Whose house is this?*
>2. *Is Solomon glad?*

I Kings 6:11

629

G. WHITE LEWIS ARCHT.
O. A. SEXMER

OLOMON IS STANDING in front of God['s] house. See all of the people who hav[e] come to have a big party because the[y] are so glad that God's house has bee[n] built! Now it is all finished and Solomon is praying. He [is] standing there with his hands raised before Heaven tall[k]ing to God. He is thanking God for being so kind to hi[m] and to his people and to his father David. He is askin[g] God to take care of them and help them all the time. Go[d] is listening. God says he will take care of the people a[s] long as they do what He tells them.

QUESTIONS:

1. Why have all the people come to God['s] house?
2. What is Solomon doing?
3. Is God listening?
4. What does God say?

I Kings 8:22-[ ]

180

WHAT A SAD THING is happening! Solomon the great king God loves is bad. He is praying to someone else. He is praying to that thing sitting there. A man made it and it is not even alive. It is called an idol. Solomon is praying to it. It cannot hear Solomon's prayer because it is not alive. God in Heaven is watching Solomon. He is very angry about this. God says that now Solomon must be punished. Poor Solomon! Why did he do such a wrong thing? I wish he had remembered to love God and had never prayed to the idol.

QUESTIONS:

1. *Is Solomon praying to God?*
2. *Where is God?*
3. *Will God punish Solomon?*

I Kings 11:1-1

THIS MAN IS ELIJAH. He is a great friend God's. Elijah is good but other peo] tried to hurt him. Elijah asked God stop it from raining for a long, long tin God listened to Elijah and stopped all the rain. Now t king is angry at Elijah for asking God to do this. Elijah afraid of the king and runs away and is sitting here b little river. There is no food here for him and no sto] where he can buy it so God is sending him some. T birds are bringing food to him. God is taking care of] friend Elijah.

QUESTIONS:

1. *What did Elijah ask God to do to the rain?*
2. *Why is he hiding?*
3. *How is Elijah getting food?*

I Kings 17:

HIS LITTLE BOY was out playing. Then he began to feel sick. After a while his mother put him into his bed but he didn't get any better. Then the little boy died. His mother asks Elijah to make him alive again. Elijah could not make the little boy alive unless God told him to. Elijah asks God to make the little boy alive and all better again. In this picture you can see what happened when Elijah prayed. The little boy is all right and Elijah is giving him to his happy mother.

QUESTIONS:

1. *What happened to the little boy?*
2. *Who did the boy's mother ask to help?*
3. *What is happening in the picture?*

I Kings 17:17-2

I N THIS PICTURE you can see Elijah prayin to God. He is asking God to send fire fror Heaven to light the big sticks he has pile on the stones. Do you see the stones an the sticks? Suddenly a great flame of fire comes sweepin down from the sky. God sent the fire because Elijah aske him to. The fire is burning the sticks. How frightene and surprised God's enemies are as they watch. They di not know that God would answer Elijah's prayer. Bu Elijah is not surprised. He knew that God would hea him. Now all the people know that the Lord is the onl God.

QUESTIONS:

1. *Where is the fire coming from?*
2. *Did God hear Elijah's prayer?*

I Kings 18:20-3

ELIJAH IS GOING UP to Heaven. His friend Elisha is watching on the ground. They were walking along together when all of a sudden this chariot of fire came down from Heaven and took Elijah up to God. Elisha sees him go. He is picking up Elijah's coat. Now Elisha will not be able to talk to Elijah any more but he can still talk to God. God is with Elisha and talks to him and makes him strong.

QUESTIONS:

1. *Who is in the fiery chariot?*
2. *Where is he going?*
3. *What is the name of the man who is picking up the coat?*

II Kings 2:1-15

DO YOU SEE THIS LADY and her two boys? She must pay some money to a man tomorrow, or the man will take her two boys away from her. He will make them come and live in his house and work hard. Elisha tells her to get all the jars and pans that she can find. He tells her to take the little jar of oil she has in her hand and pour it out into the other jars. She keeps pouring it out but her little jar never gets empty! The oil in it fills all the big jars. See how many big jars she has already filled up. She will sell the oil and get enough money to pay the man so that she can keep her children. God never let the little jar get empty.

QUESTIONS:

1. *Why was the lady sad?*
2. *What did Elisha tell her to do?*
3. *Why doesn't the little jar get empty?*

II Kings 4:1-

HIS LADY IS WAVING GOOD-BY to her hus band. He is going away. He is sick. The girl sitting there told him about God and about God's friend Elisha. The girl said that Elisha could make the sick man well again. He going away to find Elisha and to ask Elisha to make him well. Elisha will ask God to help and then the man will be all well again. It was nice for the little girl to tell the man and the lady about God. The man did not know about God until the little girl told him.

QUESTIONS:

1. *What did the little girl tell the man and the lady?*
2. *Where is the man going?*

II Kings 5:1-

THIS IS THE MAN we saw in the last pictur
when he was going away. He has come t
ask Elisha to make him well again. He
talking to Elisha. Elisha says to go dow
to the Jordan River and sit down in it seven times an
then he will be well. At first the man doesn't want to d
this. He thinks it is a funny way to get well. But soon h
goes to the river. One, two, three, four, five, six, seve
times he sits down in the river and then he is well agai
He brings presents for Elisha to pay for making hi
well, but Elisha says, "No." Elisha doesn't want h
money.

QUESTIONS:

1. *Who is this man who is standing up?*
2. *What does Elisha tell him to do?*
3. *Does Elisha want his money?*

II Kings 5:9-

ELISHA IS SITTING on top of his house. He[ ]watching some angels up in the sky. Th[ ]have come to help him and the boy who[ ]there with him. Some bad people want[ ]hurt Elisha so God sends these helpers. They won't [ ]anybody hurt Elisha and his friend.

QUESTIONS:

1. *What is happening in this picture?*
2. *Can we always see the angels?*
3. *Are there any angels here in this room?*

II Kings 6:13[ ]

THIS LITTLE BOY is seven years old but he is already the king over God's people. God has said that everyone must mind him. He has helpers so that he will know what to do. The little boy's name is Jehoash and he loves God very much. The people are happy because he their king. When he grows older he will notice that God house needs to be fixed up and he will fix it. I am sorry to say that when he becomes a big man he won't love God so much. Then he will pray to idols. What a sad thing to happen! When you get big I hope that you will only love God and pray to Him. The little boy in the picture will be very sad after he forgets about God.

QUESTIONS:

1. *How old is the little king?*
2. *Will he still love God when he grows up?*
3. *How old are you?*
4. *Do you want to love God?*

II Kings 11:1-

ING HEZEKIAH IS CRYING OUT TO GOD for help. He got a letter in the mail from a man who said that he was going to bring a lot of soldiers to catch him. King Hezekiah is very sad and doesn't know what to do. So he comes to God's house to pray and to ask God about it. He is saying, "O Lord, save me and my people! Show everyone how strong You are and that You are our God." God hears King Hezekiah praying. He will send a man soon to tell him that God will help. God will answer Hezekiah's prayer and take care of him.

QUESTIONS:

1. *Why is the king sad?*
2. *Who is he talking to?*
3. *Does God hear King Hezekiah?*

II Kings 19:1-2

202

THE MAN SITTING ON THE CHAIR is another of God's kings. His name is Josiah. He became king when he was just a little boy eight years old. Now he is grown up into a big man. See how surprised he looks! Someone is showing him a Book that he has found in God's house. It is part of the Bible. The king has never seen the Bible before and did not know what God wanted. Now he will begin to do whatever God says because he has found God's Book and can read it.

QUESTIONS:

1. *Why is the king surprised?*
2. *Where did the man find God's Book?*
3. *Do you have a Book that tells what God says?*
4. *What is the name of the Book?*

II Chronicles 34:18-28

THESE PEOPLE ARE ALL CRYING because they have done such bad things. The man who is talking to them is Ezra. He is one of God's friends so he knows what God wants them to do. Do you know what they have done? These men have married ladies who do not know about God. These ladies want God's people to pray to sticks and stones instead of to God. This is very wrong. Ezra tell the men how bad it is for them to marry ladies who don't love God. God does not want them to marry ladies who do not love Him. Now these men are sorry for what they have done. We should never marry anybody who doe not love the Lord Jesus.

QUESTIONS:

1. *What did these men do?*
2. *Can you guess what Ezra is reading to the men?*

Ezra 10:1-1

206

THE MAN IN THIS PICTURE, who doesn't have any shirt on, is named Job. He was very rich. He had many sheep and cows. Then he lost all his money and animals. Now Job is very sick and sad. Satan has taken away all of his cows and camels and all of his boys and girls so that he doesn't have anything left. Now he is very, very poor. Job is sorry but he does not blame God. He says, "God, You are good and I love You no matter what happens to me."

QUESTIONS:

1. *What is this man's name?*
2. *What happened to all of his cows?*
3. *Does Job still love God?*

Job 1:1-

208

HAVE YOU SEEN THIS MAN BEFORE? Yes, t[his] is Job, the man who became so poor a[nd] sick and now he is all right again. God h[as] given him more than he had before. [He] has more cows and more sheep and more money. J[ob] knows that God is good. Job loves God and God loves J[ob]. Do you love God like Job did? Will you do what G[od] says even if God gives you no presents? I hope you w[ill] always love God more and more because God loves y[ou] so much.

QUESTIONS:

1. *What is the name of this man?*
2. *Has God made him rich again?*

Job 42:10

HIS IS A MAN whose name is Isaiah. G[o] sent him to tell the people what th[e] should do. He is called a prophet. Ca[n] you say "prophet"? The people are ba[d] and God sends him to tell them to stop. He says that they don't, God will hurt their country, and wreck the cities, and burn up their houses. God is sorry when H[is] people sin and do wrong things. God sends Isaiah help them stop doing what is bad.

QUESTIONS:

1. *What is this man's name?*
2. *What did he tell the people?*

Isaia[h]

LOOK AT THE LITTLE CHILD. Do you see the animals that are with him? He touching the cow. A big lion is standi quietly beside him. The lion does not hu him. Do you see the little lamb, and the black wolf b hind the lamb? The wolf does not eat the lamb or hu it. Some day God will make everything happy. He w make cats and dogs like each other instead of chasi each other. The children will not quarrel and nothi will hurt them. God will make everything want to kind and gentle.

QUESTIONS:

1. *Will the lion hurt the little child?*
2. *What is God going to do some day to the c and dogs?*

Isaiah 11:1

THIS MAN IS JEREMIAH. Can you say "Jeremiah"? He is one of God's friends. God has sent him to tell the people to be good. The people do not like Jeremiah to tell them this. They want to be bad so they have tied Jeremiah's hands together. They will put him in a room and lock the door so Jeremiah cannot get away. He must sit there all day. People go by laughing at him and making fun of him. Poor Jeremiah! But God is with him and God will punish the people who do this to His friend.

QUESTIONS:

1. *What has happened to Jeremiah's hands?*
2. *Is Jeremiah God's friend?*
3. *Will God help Jeremiah?*

Jeremiah 20:1

216

HERE IS ANOTHER PICTURE of Jeremiah. Do you remember seeing him in the last picture? Jeremiah is talking to another man who is writing down all the things that Jeremiah tells him to. God is talking to Jeremiah and telling him what to say to the man, and the man is writing it down. He is writing down what God says. He is writing part of the Bible. The Bible is what God says and wants us to know. When the man has finished writing the Book he will read it to all the people, so they will know what God wants them to do.

QUESTIONS:

1. *What is Jeremiah doing?*
2. *Who is telling Jeremiah what to say?*
3. *What is the man doing who is sitting down?*

Jeremiah 36:1-4

I N THE LAST PICTURE do you remember how Jeremiah listened to God and told a man what to write? When it was all written down, God said to take it to the king so he would know what God said. The king read some of it. It said for him to be good and to stop doing bad things. The king is very angry. He does not want to mind God. Oh, oh, do you see what a terrible thing he is doing? He is throwing God's letter into the fire. He is burning it up. He does not want to have God's letter. Oh, how much God will have to punish this king because he will not listen to God or mind Him!

QUESTIONS:

1. *Who is this man?*
2. *What is he doing?*
3. *What will happen to the king because he is doing this?*

Jeremiah 36:19-24

HERE IS A SAD PICTURE. It is a picture of God's people being taken away to another country. They are going away from their homes. They want to go home but they can't. The people who are taking them away do not like them and will hurt them and kill some of them. See how sorry the people are! Do you know why this has happened? It is because they are God's people and they are bad, and God is going to punish them. They have prayed to sticks and rocks and the sun instead of praying to God. Instead of spanking them, God takes them away to another country where they don't want to go. In the picture you can see them going away.

QUESTIONS:

1. *Are the people going home?*
2. *Why is this happening?*

Jeremiah 39:1-10

THIS MAN'S NAME IS JONAH. He is running away from God. God has told him to go to a big city and tell the people there to stop being bad. Jonah is afraid to go. He is afraid the people will hurt him if he tells them what God said. So now he is running away instead of doing what God told him to. He is getting on a ship to sail far, far away to another country. He thinks God will not find him there. But nobody can run away from God. Jonah should know that. You know it, don't you?

QUESTIONS:

1. *Where is Jonah going?*
2. *Is he minding God?*
3. *What did God want Jonah to do?*

Jonah 1:1-3

224

WHO IS THIS MAN swimming in the water? I is Jonah. He was in that boat and a bi storm came along. All the men in the boa prayed to God to help them. They aske God to keep their boat from sinking. Then Jonah tol them to throw him into the water and the storm would g away. He said he was running away from God and tha God had sent the storm to punish him. The men wer sad, but they did what Jonah said and threw him out o the boat into the water and now the storm is going away Jonah is in the water but God won't let him die. He ha sent a great fish to swallow Jonah without hurting him Do you see the fish? After three days this fish will swin over to the beach with Jonah inside and spit Jonah ou onto the sand. After that Jonah will do whatever God tel him to.

QUESTIONS:

1. *Why is Jonah in the water?*
2. *What is the fish going to do?*
3. *How long will Jonah be inside the fish?*

Jonah 1:3-

HERE IS ANOTHER PICTURE of Jonah, the man who ran away from God and was swallowed by a big fish. After the fish had spit him out onto the dry ground, God spoke again to Jonah and told him to go to the city of Nineveh and to preach to the people there. "Jonah," God said, "tell the people who live in Nineveh that they have been bad and I will need to punish them next month." Here in this picture you can see Jonah doing what God told him to. He is telling all the people what God said. The people are listening. They are sorry and afraid. Now they will stop doing bad things because they know God will punish them if they keep on doing them. Now God will not need to punish these people because they are listening to Jonah. Aren't you glad that Jonah did not try to run away again?

QUESTIONS:

1. What is Jonah telling the people?

2. What are the people doing?

3. Will God need to punish these people now?

Jonah 3:1-

OW I AM GOING TO TELL you a very won‍derful story about a boy named Danie‍. The king has sent some very good food fo‍ Daniel to eat, but Daniel won't eat it. I‍ the picture you can see him telling the two men to tak‍ the food away. Shall I tell you why? Daniel doesn't wan‍ to eat the good food because the king doesn't believe i‍ God. The king prays to sticks and stones and idols. Whe‍ the king asks the blessing at the table, he doesn't ask Go‍ to bless the food. Instead the king prays to sticks an‍ stones and ugly idols and asks them to bless it. Danie‍ doesn't want to eat that kind of food, even if it is cake an‍ candy and ice cream. Daniel wants God to be happy‍ more than he wants to eat. Daniel would rather have oa‍ meal or soup from God than to have cake from the ba‍ king.

QUESTIONS:

       1. Who is this man?
       2. What is happening in this picture?

Daniel 1:3-‍

HE KING HAS MANY FRIENDS with him eating lots of good food. But do you see something very strange in this picture? Can you see where Daniel is pointing? Do you see the hand on the wall writing strange letters? No one is there, only a hand. Where does the hand come from? It must be an angel's hand, or perhaps the hand of God that is writing these letters. The king does not know what they mean. Daniel is pointing to the letters and reading them to the king. Daniel tells the king that God is angry and that the king can't be the king any more. God won't let him.

QUESTIONS:

1. Whose hand is writing the letters on the wall?
2. Who is telling the king what the letters mean?

Daniel 5:1-17

DANIEL IS PRAYING. That is good because God is hearing his prayer and will do what Daniel asks. But do you see the men hiding outside Daniel's door? What are they doing there? They are listening to Daniel. They want to know whether he is praying to God. They say that Daniel must not pray to God. They will hurt him if he does. Daniel knows the men are there listening but he does not care. He prays to God anyway. He would rather pray to God even if the men hurt him.

QUESTIONS:

1. *What is Daniel doing?*
2. *What are the men doing?*

Daniel 6:1-

HE MEN HAVE PUT DANIEL in with all of these lions. Why did they do this? It is because Daniel was praying to God. The men did not want him to pray so they put him by these lions. They thought the lions would eat Daniel up. Are the lions hurting him? No, they like Daniel. God has sent His angels to take care of him. The angels keep the lions' mouths shut so that they cannot hurt Daniel. He prays to God and God is taking care of him.

QUESTIONS:

1. *Why is Daniel there with the lions?*
2. *Will the lions hurt him?*

Daniel 6:10-23

The New Testament
in Pictures for Little Eyes

I T IS NIGHTTIME and these men are out in the fields taking care of their sheep. They chase the bears away so that they will not eat the sheep. Can you see their sheep? But now what is happening? Who are these angels who have come? What are they saying? They are telling these men that God's Son has been born that night. He is a little baby. The angels are glad and the men are glad. They go quickly to the place where the baby is, so that they can pray to Him and thank God for Him.

QUESTIONS:

1. *Why are the men outside at night?*
2. *What are the angels telling them?*
3. *What do they decide to do?*

Luke 2:1-1.

HE MEN WHO WERE TAKING CARE of the sheep have come to find God's Son. The angels told them where to find Him and now they have come to see the baby Jesus. There is the baby and His mother. The mother's name is Mary. God is the baby's Father. The men who are taking care of the sheep are worshiping the baby and thanking God that the baby is God's Son. The baby's name is Jesus.

QUESTIONS:

1. *Who is this baby?*
2. *Who is the baby's Father?*
3. *What is His mother's name?*

Luke 2:16-1

HO ARE THESE MEN? They are riding on camels. Have you ever seen a camel? Where are the men going in such a hurry? They are going to find God's Son. God has told them that His Son is going to be born. They are bringing many gifts to give Him. They know where to go because God has sent a star for them to follow. The star will take them to the baby Jesus.

QUESTIONS:

1. *Where are the men going?*
2. *How do they know where to go?*
3. *What is the name of God's Son?*

Matthew 2:1-9

244

HE MEN WHO WERE ON THE CAMELS have come a long way from another country. Now they have found the little baby they were looking for. They know that the baby is God's Son. They have brought many gifts to give Him. They are holding them out for Him to see while they worship Him and thank God. God is kind to these men to let them see His Son Jesus.

QUESTIONS:

1. *Are the men giving presents to the baby Jesus?*
2. *Can you see one of the camels?*

Matthew 2:10, 1

AN YOU SEE THE OLD MAN in the picture who is holding the baby? He has waited all his life to see God's baby Son. The old man has asked Mary if he can hold Jesus. He has never been so happy in all his life before, because now at last Jesus is born and he can hold Him in his arms. He knows that Jesus will take care of God's people. The name of the lady standing behind him is Anna. God has told her, too, that this baby is His Son and she is very very happy.

QUESTIONS:

1. *Why are the man and the lady so happy?*
2. *Is Jesus God's Son?*

Luke 2:25-38

HIS IS ANOTHER PICTURE of Jesus. He has become a big boy now. In this picture we see the big men He is talking to. These old men are preachers and teachers. The boy Jesus is asking them questions and telling them things about God. These men cannot understand how a boy can know so much about God. They do not know that this boy is God's Son. This is Jesus.

QUESTIONS:

1. Who is this boy?
2. Why are the men surprised?
3. Why does the boy know so much about God?

Luke 2:40-5.

THIS IS ANOTHER PICTURE of Jesus. Now He is a man. Another man whose name is John is pointing up to God and praying. John will baptize Jesus. Jesus is glad because God wants John to do this. As soon as Jesus is baptized He will hear a voice from the sky saying, "This is my Son and I love Him. Listen to what He tells you to do." Do you know where the voice will come from? It will be God talking to Jesus and the other people who are watching him. God wants everyone to know that this is His Son.

QUESTIONS:

    1. *What is John doing to Jesus?*
    2. *Where will the voice come from?*
    3. *What will the voice say?*

Matthew 3:13-17

JESUS HAS GONE FAR AWAY. There are no other people here to help Him or to make Him happy. He is alone. He has not eaten anything for breakfast, or lunch, or supper. He did not eat anything yesterday or the day before that. He has not eaten anything for forty days. Soon Satan, God's enemy, will come and try to get Jesus to do something bad but Jesus will not listen to bad Satan. Jesus is God's Son and He is good. He has never done anything bad at all. He will never listen to Satan. Jesus listens only to God His Father and does only what God says.

QUESTIONS:

1. *Why is Jesus hungry?*
2. *Will He ever do anything bad?*
3. *Who will try to get Jesus to be bad?*

Matthew 4:1-11

ESUS ASKS TWELVE MEN to be His special friends. These men are called His disciples. They go with Jesus wherever He goes and help Him in all His work. These men are happy because Jesus has asked them to help Him. Some of the names of these men are Peter, John, James, Thomas, and Andrew. These twelve men are Jesus' helpers.

QUESTIONS:

1. *Who are these men?*
2. *Will they help Jesus?*
3. *Do you know any of their names?*

Mark 3:13-19

NE DAY JESUS was at a big dinner where a lady was getting married. After a while they needed more grape juice for the people to drink. They ask Jesus what to do. Jesus tells them to fill up six big jars of water and tells them to take them to the man. And do you know what? It wasn't water any more. It was better than they had ever tasted. Jesus can do things like that because He is God.

QUESTIONS:

1. *What did the people ask Jesus to do?*
2. *What did Jesus tell them to do with the big jars?*
3. *Can Jesus help us when we need Him?*

John 2:1-1

ESUS IS MAKING SOME MEN go out of th
church. They didn't come to church t
love God and pray. No, they are doin
things there that God does not want the
to do. They are selling things to get a lot of money an
be rich. They don't love God and don't want to pra
Jesus has a whip in His hand and the men are afraid c
Him. He tells them to take all of those things away. H
says that they are in His Father's house and they mu:
not do things like that when they are there.

QUESTIONS:

1. *What does Jesus have in His hand?*
2. *What does Jesus want these men to do?*

John 2:13-

DO YOU SEE JESUS standing there? He told Peter to throw his fishing net in the water. Peter did not think that there would be any fish but he did what Jesus told him to do, and now just see how many fish there are! Peter minded Jesus and now Peter has all these fish. Can you see all the fish? There are almost too many to count. Peter and his friends don't know what to do with all of them. They have so many in their boat that it is almost sinking. They give some to the men in the other boat and it is almost sinking too. Where did all these fish come from?

QUESTIONS:

1. *Who told Peter to catch the fish?*
2. *Can you count how many fish there are, or are there too many?*

Luke 5:1-1

WHAT IS HAPPENING HERE? Look at the men at the top of the picture. They brought their friend to Jesus. They have taken away part of the roof of the house and put him down right in front of Jesus where He will be sure to see him. The man could not walk and was lying on his bed. Can you see his bed? They brought him to Jesus because they want him to walk again. Jesus tells the man to get well and now he is standing up. He has already learned to walk. Jesus makes him well right away.

QUESTIONS:

1. *How did the men get their friend down to Jesus?*
2. *Could the man walk before?*
3. *What did Jesus do?*

Luke 5:17-20

IT IS NIGHTTIME and Jesus is talking to man whose name is Nicodemus. Can yo say, "Nicodemus"? He is a good man bu he does not know that Jesus is God's So and he doesn't know very much about God. Jesus is telling him about God. He is telling him how to get t Heaven. He says, "Nicodemus, you cannot get there b yourself but God will take you there if you believe in M God loves you, Nicodemus." Jesus died so that Nicode mus could go to Heaven. Jesus died so that you and I ca go to Heaven if we love Him.

QUESTIONS:

1. *What is this man's name?*
2. *Did he know God?*
3. *Why did Jesus have to die?*

John 3:1-5, 14-

HIS MAN IS GLAD because his little boy feels all better again. Yesterday he was so sick that he didn't want to run and play. He only wanted to be there in his bed. His father was sad. He went to see Jesus. He asked Jesus to come and make the little boy well. Jesus said that He would help. He told the father to go home and the little boy would be all right. Jesus is far away but He makes the little boy well again.

QUESTIONS:

1. Was the little boy sick?
2. Is he sick now?
3. Where is Jesus?

John 4:46-5

ESUS IS TALKING TO THE PEOPLE. See how many of them there are! They want to hear what Jesus says. They know Jesus is their Friend and they want to mind Him. He is telling the people to be kind and good. He tells them not to quarrel. Some of these people will love Jesus always and some of them will go away from Him and not want Him to be their Friend any more. Isn't that too bad? If Jesus is not their Friend, then God will not let them come to Heaven. Jesus wants to be your Friend too.

QUESTIONS:

       1. Who is talking to the people?
       2. Is Jesus your Friend?

Matthew 5:1-11

ESUS TOLD A STORY about two men who built houses. One of them built his house on the sand. He was a foolish man. It rained and rained and all of the sand washed away and the house fell down. The other man built his house upon a rock. Even though it rains the rock will not wash away. He is a wise man because he built his house upon a rock.

QUESTIONS:

1. *Was it a good idea to build a house on the sand?*
2. *What happened to that house?*
3. *When it rained did the house on the rock fall down?*

Matthew 7:24-29

ESUS IS HELPING A MAN SIT UP. The man was dead and his mother was sad. Jesus saw the mother crying. He went over to see the man lying on the bed. The man could not move. He was dead. Jesus tells him to be alive again. When Jesus says that, all of a sudden the man begins to move. He opens his eyes and sees Jesus and he sees his mother too. The man and his mother are glad and Jesus is glad too.

QUESTIONS:

1. *Was the man dead?*
2. *What did Jesus tell him to do?*
3. *Then what happened?*

Luke 7:11-

ESUS AND HIS FRIENDS are in a boat. It i at night. There is a great storm. The wind is blowing. It is raining hard. Th friends are afraid the ship will sink and they will all be drowned. Is Jesus afraid? No, He isn't. No because He knows His God will take care of them. Jesu is standing up and holding up His hands and now the storm is going away. Jesus tells the storm to stop and i did.

QUESTIONS:

1. *Is Jesus afraid?*
2. *What is He doing?*
3. *What will happen to the storm?*

Matthew 8:23-2

THIS LITTLE GIRL is twelve years old. She was very sick and her father went to find Jesus. He asked Jesus to come and make his little girl well again. The doctors couldn't get her better, but he knows Jesus can. Jesus comes and takes the little girl's hand and says, "Get up, little girl." Right away she sits up and gets out of bed and starts to play and she is all right again. The little girl died but Jesus brought her back to life and gave her to her mother and father. That is why they are so surprised and happy.

QUESTIONS:

1. *Why are the mother and father so happy?*
2. *How did Jesus make the little girl well?*

Mark 5:22-4

ESUS IS TALKING here with a man who cannot see Him. The man is blind. His eyes are hurt so that he cannot see anything at all. Close your eyes now and you can tell what it is like to be blind. Everything is dark. Someone told this man Jesus was coming. The man heard Jesus coming. Then he cried out very loudly, "Jesus, please help me. Please make my eyes well so that I can see." Jesus touches his eyes and says, "Be open." And right away his eyes are all right and he can see. Isn't Jesus a wonderful Friend?

QUESTIONS:

1. *Could the man see Jesus?*
2. *What did Jesus say to make his eyes open?*

Matthew 9:27-31

280

THIS POOR MAN lying on the ground was going on a trip, and all of a sudden some men came and took away his money and some of his clothes and hurt him and ran away. They left him lying there on the road. Some people he knew came walking by but they wouldn't stop to help him. They just looked at him and went on. Then a man he didn't like came along and stopped. You can see him in the picture helping the poor man who is hurt. He is pouring some medicine on some places and soon he will lift him up and put him on his donkey and take him to a hotel. Jesus wants us to be kind to everyone, even people who hit us or don't like us.

QUESTIONS:

1. *Why is the man lying there?*
2. *What is the other man doing?*

Luke 10:30-37

MARY IS SITTING DOWN listening while Jesus is talking to her. He is telling her many things that she needs to know. Do you see the other lady, the one who is standing up? Her name is Martha. She is Mary's sister. She is getting supper ready. Martha is working very hard and wants Mary to help her instead of talking to Jesus. Martha asks Jesus to make Mary help her get the supper. But Jesus says, "No, let Mary sit here and listen, because that is even more important than getting supper." Did you know that it is more important to listen to Jesus than it is to eat?

QUESTIONS:

1. *Who are these two ladies?*
2. *What does the one standing up want the other one to do?*
3. *Did Jesus say that Mary should keep on listening to Him?*

Luke 10:38-42

284

ESUS IS ANGRY with these men. He is talking to them while they are eating their dinners. He is angry because they say that they love God and they really don't. They say that they want to mind God, but they are telling lies because they want to do things their own way instead of the way God says. They give money to God but they do not love Him. They go to God's house but they do not love God. That is why Jesus is angry. He wants them to love God. He does not want their money unless they love Him.

QUESTIONS:

1. *Why is Jesus angry with these men?*
2. *Do these men love God?*
3. *Do they give money to God?*
4. *Does God want their money if they do not love Him?*

Luke 11:37-44

THIS MAN IS A RICH FARMER. He has lots of money. He is looking at his barns. Do you see his men putting hay into the barns? But this man does not love God. He loves his money and his farm more than he loves God. He has so much money and food that he doesn't know where to put it so he is going to build a bigger barn. But tonight God will let this rich man die so he will not wake up tomorrow morning. He can't use all his food in the barn any more because he will die tonight and never come back. God will take him away. The man is bad because he loves his farm but doesn't love God.

QUESTIONS:

1. *Does this man have lots of things?*
2. *Does this man love God?*

Luke 12:16-21

ESUS IS TALKING to His friends. Do you see the pretty flower He is pointing to? Jesus is telling them to look at the flowers. The flowers don't work hard to cook their suppers, do they? No, flowers don't need to cook and work hard, because God takes care of them. They don't need fine clothes, because God has made them grow with their beautiful clothes right on them. Jesus is telling His friends that God takes care of the flowers and He will take care of them too if they ask Him, and do whatever He says.

QUESTIONS:

1. What is Jesus showing the disciples?

2. Will God take care of you?

Luke 12:27-32

THIS MAN IS PLANTING SEEDS. He is carrying them in his bag over his shoulder. He throws the little seeds out on the ground. He wants them to grow and become soft green grass. He wants them to become big plants. Oh look, do you see the birds behind him? They are eating up some of the seeds. Those seeds will not grow because the birds are taking them away. Some of the seed is falling down on the rocks and thorns. Can you see the thorns? The seeds cannot grow there very well. But some of the seeds fall on good ground and will grow up and become big plants.

QUESTIONS:

1. *Will the seed grow on the rock?*
2. *Where will the seed grow best?*

Matthew 13:3-

OOK AT ALL THESE PEOPLE. See how many there are? They are all hungry. They have not had any lunch and now it is time for supper and they don't have anything to eat. One boy brought his lunch so he will not be hungry. He would be glad to give his lunch to all the people but do you think that would be enough for them to eat? No, of course not. The boy is giving his lunch to Jesus. Jesus will break the bread in pieces and give the pieces to His helpers, and do you know what will happen then? Jesus makes the bread grow so that there will be enough for everyone.

QUESTIONS:

1. *What is the boy doing with his lunch?*
2. *What will Jesus do with it?*

Matthew 14:15-2

HAT IS HAPPENING in this picture? There is water with a boat in it and there are some men in the boat. Do you see Jesus in the picture? Is He swimming in the water? No, He is walking on top of it. Can you walk on top of water in your bathtub? No, of course not. But Jesus made the water. He can stand on it if He wants to. One of the men in the boat is Peter. When Peter sees Jesus on the water he wants to walk on it too. Peter will step out on the water and start to walk toward Jesus. Then he will become frightened and begin to sink, and Jesus will come and save him.

QUESTIONS:

1. *Can Jesus walk on top of the water?*
2. *Will Peter walk part of the way on top of the water?*
3. *When Peter gets scared, then what will happen?*

Matthew 14:22-33

296

JESUS IS TALKING to Peter and James and John. They are up on a high mountain. No one else is there. All of a sudden Jesus' clothes begin to shine and become brighter and brighter, and whiter than snow. Peter and James and John are frightened. Then all of a sudden they see two other men standing there talking to Jesus. You can see them there in the picture. These two men are Moses and Elijah who lived long ago. They have come down from Heaven to talk to Jesus. They are talking about how some bad men are going to take Jesus and hurt Him and kill Him. Soon Moses and Elijah will go away again and a bright cloud will come over above where Jesus is standing. God's voice will talk out of the cloud and say, "Jesus is My Son, listen to Him."

QUESTIONS:

1. *What color did Jesus' clothes become?*
2. *Who came to talk with Jesus?*
3. *What did the voice in the cloud say?*

Matthew 17:1-9

AZARUS IS JESUS' FRIEND. One day Lazarus got sick and died. Jesus wasn't there to make him well again. The friends of Lazarus took his body and put it in the hole in the big rock and covered the hole so that no one could go in or out. When Jesus came he told the men to roll away the stone, and Jesus prayed and asked God to make Lazarus alive. Now can you see what is happening in this picture? Lazarus is coming out again. He was dead but now he is alive. Do you know why? It is because Jesus is there.

QUESTIONS:

1. *Did Jesus make the man alive?*
2. *Are the people glad that Jesus came?*

John 11:1-45

ESUS LOVES LITTLE CHILDREN. In this picture He is holding some of them on His lap and talking to them. Once Jesus' friends tried to send the children away. They thought that Jesus didn't want children around Him. Jesus talked to the disciples and told them never to say things like that. He wants the children to be with Him. He says, "Let the little children come to Me. Do not send them away because I love them and want them with Me."

QUESTIONS:

1. *What is Jesus holding in His arms?*
2. *Does Jesus love little children?*
3. *Are you a little child?*
4. *Does Jesus love you?*

Matthew 19:13-15

ESUS IS CRYING. He is looking at the old city of Jerusalem. There are many people in this city where He is looking. They do not love Jesus or His Father. They do not know that Jesus is God's Son. Jesus knows that some day a great army will come and knock down their city. If these people would only believe in Jesus then these terrible things would not happen to them. Jesus loves them and wants to help them, but they do not love Jesus and that is why He is crying.

QUESTIONS:

1. *What is Jesus looking at?*
2. *Why is He crying?*

Luke 13:31-35

HE MAN IN THE PICTURE has lost one of his sheep. It ran away and fell down and couldn't get back up again. The little sheep is lost and crying and helpless. The man went to find him and finally he is there picking it up. He will take it home and get it all warm again and get it something to eat. The man in the picture is good because he takes care of the sheep. The man looks like Jesus. Jesus wants to take care of us when we get lost. Jesus loves you very much. You can be one of His little lambs.

QUESTIONS:

1. *How did the little sheep get there?*
2. *What is the man doing?*

Luke 15:3-7

306

THIS LADY IS PUTTING PERFUME on Jesus' feet and then wiping it off with her hair. The perfume has cost a lot of money. The men sitting at the table with Jesus are telling Him that the lady shouldn't do this but Jesus is glad. He wants her to use the perfume because she is doing it to tell Jesus, "Thank You." Jesus has been kind to her. She has done many bad things but Jesus will forgive her. Jesus will die for her sins. She is glad that He is so kind and so she has put the perfume on His feet to tell Him, "Thank You." Jesus died for you, too. Have you told Him, "Thank You"?

QUESTIONS:

1. *Where did the lady put the perfume?*
2. *Was Jesus glad?*
3. *Have you ever told Jesus, "Thank You," for what He has done for you?*
4. *Shall we thank Him now?*

John 12:1-7

THIS BOY IS GOING AWAY from home. He is saying good-by to his father. Now he will jump on his horse and ride away. His father is sorry because he doesn't want the boy to go away. But the boy thinks it will be more fun away from home. He asks his father to give him a lot of money and now he will go away. Are you sorry that the boy is so bad? He should have stayed at home and worked and helped his father instead of going away.

QUESTIONS:

1. *Did the boy want to stay home or go away?*
2. *Is the father happy or sad?*

Luke 15:11-19

IN THIS PICTURE you can see the man who went away from his house even when his father didn't want him to. Now he has come back home again. He is sitting in a big chair and his father is very happy. After he went away he began to get very hungry and so he decided to come home again. His father is glad to see him. He didn't know if his father would want him to come back, but you can see how happy the father is to see him again. When the father saw him he ran and welcomed him and is telling him how glad he is.

QUESTIONS:

1. *Did the father let the boy come home?*
2. *Is the boy happy?*
3. *Is the father happy?*

Luke 15:20-24

O YOU SEE THESE MEN who are walking away from Jesus? They were lepers. That means that they were very sick. Everyone was afraid to go near them because they were so sick. People who touched them might get sick too. When they saw Jesus they called to Him and said, "Jesus, help us. Please help us." Jesus saw them and heard them calling. He wanted to help them and He made all of them well. He healed them all but only one of them came back to tell Him, "Thank You." This man is so glad he is well again that he falls down in front of Jesus. All the others forgot to tell Jesus, "Thank You."

QUESTIONS:

1. *Were all these men sick?*
2. *Who healed them?*
3. *What is the man in the picture doing?*
4. *Have you thanked Jesus because He is your Friend?*

Luke 17:11-19

183-A

WHY IS THIS MAN LYING HERE so still? It is because he is dead. His father owns that house but some other people are living there. His father sent his son to get the rent money from the people staying in the house but the people wouldn't give the money to him. Instead they hurt him and killed him and threw him out on the ground where you can see him lying. What do you think the father will do when he hears about this? He will come and get the policeman, and they will catch the people who live in this house and take them off to jail, because of the terrible thing they have done to his son.

QUESTIONS:

1. *Who owns this house?*
2. *What did the man's father send him to get?*
3. *What did the people do?*

Matthew 21:33-41

JESUS IS SITTING in God's house watching the people putting money into a box. They are giving this money to God. In the picture you can see a lady who doesn't have very much money. She has brought a few pennies. That is all the money she has, and she is giving it all to God. When she puts this in she will not have any more money left at all. She is giving God everything that she has. Jesus is glad because the lady loves God so much. He doesn't think the rich men standing there have given very much at all. They have put in lots and lots of money but they are still rich and have lots more money left for themselves at home. Jesus says the poor woman's few pennies are better than all the money from the rich people who don't love Him.

QUESTIONS:

1. *Did the rich men put in a lot of money?*
2. *How much does the poor lady have left after she puts in her money?*

Mark 12:41-44

EVERYONE IS HAPPY because Jesus has come to visit them. He has come to the city of Jerusalem. All the people think he has come to Jerusalem to be their king. They want Jesus to be king because He is so kind to them and can help them. See how some people are putting their coats on the ground for Jesus to ride over. Others are cutting down branches from the trees and making a path for Him. The people shout and thank God because they think Jesus will help them all be rich and have lots of money and other things that they don't have now. They do not know that Jesus will soon be killed.

QUESTIONS:

1. *Are the people happy?*
2. *What are they putting down on the road for Jesus to ride over?*
3. *Why are they doing this?*

John 12:12-19

ERE IN THIS PICTURE you can see Jesus talking to some of His friends. He is telling them about what is going to happen to Him. He is pointing up to Heaven, telling them that soon He will go there to be with God His Father. Jesus says that some day all His friends will come to Heaven too and live there with Him always.

QUESTIONS:

1. *Where is Jesus pointing?*
2. *What is He telling His friends?*

Luke 22:14-22

THIS MAN HAS MADE a great dinner and is ready to eat it. Can you see the man pointing to the food on the table? But who is coming to eat it? The man asked many of his rich friends to come and have dinner with him but they wouldn't. They didn't know what a wonderful dinner it was going to be so they said they had other things to do and couldn't come. Then the man invited the poor people who were sick and crippled and blind. Do you see them coming? They are glad to come and eat. Soon the table will be full of people. The man is glad because of his new friends but he is sorry because of those who would not come. Jesus wants you to come and live with Him some day. Will you be glad to come?

QUESTIONS:

1. *Who did the man invite at first to come and eat the good dinner?*
2. *Did the people he asked first want to come?*
3. *Who finally came to the dinner?*
4. *Does Jesus want you to come to Him?*

Matthew 22:1-14

SOME MEN ARE ASKING Jesus a question. They want to know what is the most important rule for them to mind. Can you think what that rule would be? Would it be to eat nicely? Or would it be not going across the street alone? No. These things are very important and you should eat nicely and must be careful about cars or you will get into trouble. But there is something even more important that we should do. Jesus tells these men what it is. He says that the greatest thing for them to do is to always love God. Do you love God? Do you do whatever He says? What are some things God wants you to do?

QUESTIONS:

1. *What is the most important rule to mind?*
2. *What are some things God wants you to do?*
3. *Do you love God by doing what He says?*

Matthew 22:35-40

HAT IS HAPPENING IN this picture? Jesus has a loaf of bread in His hand. He is breaking it into pieces. He will give these pieces to His disciples who are sitting there at the supper table. Jesus will tell them to eat the bread. He says that the bread is His body. Jesus is telling His disciples that He must soon die. He died for you. He died for me. We have done bad things that God must punish. But Jesus asked to be punished for you. God punished Jesus instead of you. Jesus didn't do anything bad but God punished Him. Do you know why?

QUESTIONS:

1. *What does Jesus have in His hand?*
2. *Who will eat the bread?*
3. *What is going to happen to Jesus?*

Luke 22:14-20

ESUS IS TALKING to His disciples. He is telling them what is going to happen to Him. Some men are going to take Him and kill Him but Jesus tells them not to be afraid. He says that God will take care of them. Jesus tells them that He will go away to His Father, away up in Heaven. When He gets there He will get places ready for them to come to live. He is getting a place ready for you to live in Heaven too, if you love Jesus.

QUESTIONS:

1. *What is Jesus telling them?*
2. *Where is Jesus now?*

John 14:1-14

ESUS IS PRAYING all alone. He is in a garden and it is night. He is talking to His Father in Heaven. Jesus is very, very sad because He knows what will happen to Him soon. He knows that some men will come to get Him and take Him away and nail Him to a cross so that He will die. He will die on the cross so that God will not need to punish you and me for the bad things we have done. Jesus is sad because He does not want to die. He doesn't need to, either. He could ask God to send the angels to take care of Him but He will let the men kill Him. Jesus is glad to die for you.

QUESTIONS:

1. *Is Jesus happy or sad?*
2. *What is going to happen to Him?*

Luke 22:39-48

H. Hofmann

DID YOU EVER HEAR about a man named Judas Iscariot? Judas pretended that he was one of Jesus' friends. Some bad men said they would give Judas lots of money if he would help them catch Jesus. In this picture Judas is bringing them to where Jesus is. It is night. They are bringing torches. Do you see the torches in their hands, giving light? They don't have flashlights and so they use these torches instead. Is Jesus going to run away from them? No, Jesus is standing, waiting. He could go away if He wanted to, but He will let them take Him.

QUESTIONS:

1. *What is the name of the man leading these bad people to Jesus?*
2. *Why doesn't Jesus run away?*

Luke 22:47-54

ETER IS ONE of Jesus' friends and disciples. He is getting warm by being near the fire with some other people. Peter looks angry. The lady is pointing at him but he is telling this lady, "No." Why is he saying that? This lady has asked Peter if Jesus is his Friend. Peter tells her, "No." He says that he doesn't know Jesus at all. What a bad thing to say. Peter is telling a lie because he is afraid the other people there will hurt him if they know he is Jesus' friend. Soon he will look up and see Jesus looking at him and then he will cry because he has done such a bad thing.

QUESTIONS:

1. Was Peter a friend of Jesus?
2. What did Peter tell the girl?

John 18:10-27

OW THE PEOPLE HAVE TAKEN JESUS to a man whose name was Pilate. Pilate can let them kill Jesus or else make them let Jesus go. He is talking to the people and telling them that he thinks he ought to let Jesus go. He says Jesus is good. He tells them that Jesus hasn't done anything bad at all. See how angry the people are! They want Pilate to let them kill Jesus. They are shouting at Pilate and Pilate is afraid of them. Soon he will decide to give Jesus to the men so that they can kill Him.

QUESTIONS:

1. *What is this man's name?*
2. *What do the people want Pilate to do?*
3. *What will Pilate do?*

John 19:1-16

173

HE BAD MEN have taken Jesus up the hill and have nailed His hands and His feet on these big pieces of wood so that He will die after a while. Can you think what it would be like if you were hanging there with nails through your hands? Oh, what a terrible thing they are doing to Jesus! Do you know why Jesus was nailed there? It is because He loves you and me. You and I have done bad things and God should punish us. But God doesn't want to do that because He loves us. God sent His dear Son Jesus who wanted to be punished for us. In this picture you can see Jesus being punished for your sins by dying there on the cross. That is how much Jesus loves you. He died for you.

QUESTIONS:

1. *What are in Jesus' hands?*
2. *Why did Jesus let them kill Him?*
3. *Does Jesus love you?*

John 19:16-24

ESUS IS DEAD. His body is all wrapped up in a white cloth. His friends are putting His body into a great hole in the rock. Soon they will leave Him there all alone. They do not think they will ever see Jesus again. They will go away and leave Him here because He is dead. How sad they are! They do not know that soon He will become alive again and come out of the place where they are putting Him. Jesus is dead but God is going to bring Him back to life.

QUESTIONS:

1. *Where are they putting Jesus' body?*
2. *Will His body stay there in the hole?*

John 19:40-42

THESE THREE LADIES are Jesus' friends. They have come to His grave to put some sweet perfume on the clothes He was wrapped up in after He died. They thought this would be a nice thing to do even though Jesus was dead and couldn't smell the perfume. Then they would sadly go away and leave Jesus there and never see Him again. But what is happening? An angel is inside the grave where Jesus was. The angel tells them Jesus isn't there! Jesus is alive and has gone away! Jesus was dead, but God made Him alive again! Jesus said this would happen, but no one believed Him. Now His friends know that whatever Jesus says is always true. He says that He will make all His friends alive again after they are dead. He will take them up to Heaven to be with Him always and always. Are you one of Jesus' friends? Aren't you glad that Jesus is alive?

QUESTIONS:

1. *Who are these three ladies?*
2. *Who is talking to them?*
3. *What is he telling them?*

Mark 16:1-8

344

A T LAST some of Jesus' friends are meeting Him again. They are very surprised. They thought Jesus was dead. They didn't know that Jesus was alive again. They are walking along and they see somebody standing there, and it is Jesus! How surprised and happy they are. They know now that Jesus is God's Son and they fall down at His feet and pray to Him. Jesus is saying, "Don't be afraid. Go and tell My other friends to go to a certain place and I will meet them there."

QUESTIONS:

1. *Who are these ladies talking to?*
2. *Why are they surprised and happy?*

John 20:11-18

DO YOU SEE THESE TWO MEN running as fast as they can? One of them is Peter and the other one is John. Peter is the older man and John is younger. Why are they running so fast? It is because the women have told them that Jesus is not in the grave but is alive again. Peter and John can hardly believe what the women have told them and they are going to see for themselves. They do not understand how Jesus could be alive and not in the hole in the rock. What an exciting morning this was when Jesus came back to life again!

QUESTIONS:

1. *Who are these two men?*
2. *Where are they going?*
3. *What will they find out?*

John 20:1-5

ETER AND JOHN ran right into the place where Jesus had been buried. In the picture you can see Peter inside, looking for Jesus. Is Jesus there? No, the cloth that was wrapped around Jesus is lying there, but Jesus has come out and gone away. He is alive again and isn't in the grave. Peter is surprised. John is surprised too. John is standing outside looking in. Finally they know that Jesus is not dead any more.

QUESTIONS:

1. Which man is Peter?
2. Where is Jesus?

John 20:6-10

THREE MEN ARE WALKING along a road. Two of them are going to their home. When the third man came along and asked them why they were so sad they said it was because Jesus was dead. The third man began to tell them more about Jesus and why He had to die. He told them that Jesus died for their sins. The two men are asking this third man to come and eat with them. While they were eating, all of a sudden they realized that the third man was Jesus. They had been talking to Jesus and didn't know it! As soon as they knew this, suddenly Jesus disappeared and wasn't eating there with them any more. He had gone away.

QUESTION:

1. Who is the third man?

Luke 24:13-32

THE DISCIPLES WERE TALKING together when all of a sudden Jesus was standing there with them. He hadn't knocked or come in at the door. He was just there! He must have come right through the walls because Jesus can do anything. His disciples were scared but Jesus says, "Don't be afraid, I am Jesus." In this picture you can see Him showing His friends the holes in His hands and His feet, so that they will know that this is really their very own Jesus who was nailed to the big pieces of wood and died. Now He is alive again and they are seeing Him. Pretty soon He will eat some fish with them and some honey, so that they will know that He is really alive and is not just a ghost.

QUESTIONS:

1. *Who is the man talking to the disciples?*
2. *Did He open the door and come in?*

Luke 24:33-48

354

NE DAY WHILE JESUS was talking with His disciples out on a hill, all of a sudden He began to go up into the air. Do you see the cloud there above Him? Jesus goes into the cloud and they will not see Him any more. Do you know where He is going? He is going to Heaven to live again with God His Father. When Jesus has gone away, two angels will come and talk with Jesus' friends and tell them that Jesus will come back again some day. Some day Jesus is going to come and take all His friends to Heaven. Are you one of Jesus' friends?

QUESTIONS:

1. *Where is Jesus going?*
2. *Will He come back again?*

Acts 1:9-11

ONE DAY WHILE JESUS' FRIENDS were praying together, there came a noise that sounded like a big wind coming from the sky, and the noise was all around them in the house, although they couldn't feel any wind. Do you see what is on the men's heads? It looks like tongues made of fire on each of them. Why is this happening? It is because God the Holy Spirit is coming down upon these men. After a while the tongues of fire will go away but the Holy Spirit will stay in their hearts. The Holy Spirit will help them and tell them many things and make them very strong. Jesus sent the Holy Spirit to comfort and help them.

QUESTIONS:

1. *What is on the men's heads?*
2. *Who is coming into these men?*
3. *Who sent the Holy Spirit to them?*

Acts 2:1-3

ETER IS TALKING to all of these other people who don't know about Jesus yet. He is telling them that Jesus wants to be their friend and their Saviour. They have come from all over the world. Peter is telling them about how Jesus died and came back to life. These people come from a different country, but Peter is talking to them in their own language. God is helping Peter and the other disciples to talk in whatever language they need to tell people about Jesus. When these people hear about Jesus dying for them they are sad and ask what they should do. Peter told them to believe on the Lord Jesus, and many of them did.

QUESTIONS:

1. What is Peter telling these people?
2. Do they decide to love Jesus?

Acts 2:4-8, 14-21

PETER AND JOHN have come to God's house to pray. A man is sitting there who can't walk. Something is the matter with his legs. He was that way when he was a tiny baby and he has never been able to walk. That is why he is sitting there near God's house asking people to give him money to buy food. When he sees Peter and John he asks them to give him some money. Peter says he didn't have any, but he could give him something else that was a lot better. He says, "Get up and walk. Jesus will make you well." In the picture you can see the man beginning to get up. He will walk and run. He will give thanks to God.

QUESTIONS:

1. *Could this man walk before Peter talked to him?*
2. *Where is Jesus?*
3. *Did Jesus help Peter make the man walk?*

Acts 3:1-11

ETER IS TALKING to the bad men who killed Jesus. They don't like Peter and would like to kill him. They are angry because Peter made the man walk, who was sitting on the steps of the church. In the picture you can see the man standing there with Peter. Peter tells them that Jesus made the man well again. They are telling Peter not to talk about Jesus any more and Peter isn't minding them. Peter minds God, but not these men, so he will keep on telling how kind and wonderful Jesus is.

QUESTIONS:

1. *Do the bad people want Peter to talk about Jesus?*
2. *Will Peter stop talking about Jesus?*

Acts 4:5-21

HE MAN LYING DOWN on the floor is dead. The man standing up is Peter. Peter was sitting there and the man came in and told him a lie. As soon as he told the lie he suddenly fell down and died. God punished Ananias because he told a lie. Soon the people will carry him outside and make a hole and put him in it and cover him up.

QUESTIONS:

1. *Why is the man there on the floor?*
2. *Did he tell a lie to God?*

Acts 5:1-11

PETER IS IN JAIL. The bad people who killed Jesus have put him there. The doors and windows are all locked so that he can't get out. He has been there all night. Here in this picture you can see Peter lying there in jail when all of a sudden an angel comes. The angel is waking Peter up and telling him to come with him. The angel will unlock the doors of the jail. The angel doesn't have a key but he will open the doors anyway. When he is safely out he will tell Peter to go and tell more people about Jesus. God sent His angel to help Peter.

QUESTIONS:

1. *Does the angel have a key to the door?*
2. *What did the angel tell Peter to do?*

Acts 12:1-17

675

OH, WHAT IS HAPPENING to this man? He is kneeling down and praying while the bad men are killing him with big stones. Is he crying? No. He is praying and asking God not to hurt these men even though they are hurting him. These men are angry because Stephen told them about Jesus. They don't want to hear about Jesus and so they decided to kill Stephen. Stephen is happy because he sees Jesus up there in Heaven. In a little while he will go there and be with Jesus.

QUESTIONS:

1. *What is the man's name?*
2. *Why are these men throwing big stones at him?*

Acts 6:8-15; 7:54-60

HE MAN SITTING in the chariot and reading the Book wants to know more about God. He is reading part of the Bible. He has stopped the horses and is talking to Philip. Philip is one of Jesus' disciples. The Holy Spirit told him to run over to the chariot and start talking to the man. He is telling the man what the Bible means. He is telling him about Jesus. Soon the man sitting in the chariot will be a Christian.

QUESTIONS:

1. *What is the man's name who is standing there?*
2. *Who is he talking about?*
3. *Will the other man become a Christian?*

Acts 8:26-40

THIS MAN'S NAME IS PAUL. He doesn't like Christians. He would like to kill all of them or put them in jail. He is walking down the road trying to find some Christians to hurt. He thinks that all Christians are bad. He does not know that Jesus is God's Son. Paul thinks God likes him to hurt Christians. But soon God will tell Paul to love Jesus and His people. Then Paul won't hurt them any more.

QUESTIONS:

1. *What is this man's name?*
2. *Why does he hurt the Christians?*

Acts 9:1, 2

ERE IS ANOTHER PICTURE of Paul. While he was walking down the road all of a sudden God started talking to him from Heaven. He is telling Paul not to hurt the Christians any more. He is saying, "Paul, you too must become one of My friends. I am Jesus, and you must stop hurting Me and you must leave My people alone." Paul is very surprised and afraid, and is asking Jesus what He wants him to do. Jesus tells him and now Paul will always do whatever Jesus says.

QUESTIONS:

1. *Who is talking to Paul?*
2. *Does Paul decide to love Jesus?*

Acts 9:3-19

WHO IS THIS MAN in the basket? It is Paul. His friends are helping him to get away. Paul has been telling everyone about his new Friend Jesus and how much he loves Him. Paul doesn't hurt God's children any more. The people who don't like God try to catch Paul so his friends are helping him to run away. Paul is God's friend now and he loves Jesus.

QUESTIONS:

1. *Who is the man in the basket?*
2. *Why is he running away?*

Acts 9:22-28

PAUL AND SILAS are in jail but they don't care very much because they know that God loves them. They don't care what happens to them so they have been singing. All of a sudden a great earthquake shakes the jail and all of the doors swing open and the chains fall off their hands and feet so that they can run away. But they are not trying to run away. They are staying there and talking to the man who is supposed to keep them in jail. He is kneeling there asking them what to do. They are telling him to believe on Jesus and he will be saved.

QUESTIONS:

1. *Where are Paul and Silas?*
2. *Who are they talking to?*
3. *What did they tell the man to do?*

Acts 16:22-34

380

PAUL IS ON A BOAT and there is a great storm. Do you see the waves and how the ship is sinking? But God took care of Paul and all the people who were with him and none of them were hurt. They came through the water and got to the shore all right. Paul is standing there telling God, "Thank You," for taking care of them. God loves Paul, and God loves you.

QUESTIONS:

1. *Did the ship sink?*
2. *Were the people saved?*
3. *Does God love you?*

Acts 27:14-44

MOODY PRESS
THE NAME YOU CAN TRUST
A MINISTRY OF MOODY BIBLE INSTITUTE

Moody Press, a ministry of the Moody Bible
Institute, is designed for education, evangelization,
and edification. If we may assist you in knowing
more about Christ and the Christian life, please
write to us without obligation:

Moody Press, c/o MLM, Chicago, Illinois 60610 USA